COHERENT SCHOOL LEADERSHIP

ASCD MEMBER BOOK

Many ASCD members received this book as a
member benefit upon its initial release.

Learn more at: **www.ascd.org/memberbooks**

Michael **FULLAN**
Lyle **KIRTMAN**

COHERENT SCHOOL LEADERSHIP

Forging Clarity
from Complexity

 Alexandria, Virginia USA

1703 N. Beauregard St. • Alexandria, VA 22311-1714 USA
Phone: 800-933-2723 or 703-578-9600 • Fax: 703-575-5400
Website: www.ascd.org • E-mail: member@ascd.org
Author guidelines: www.ascd.org/write

Ronn Nozoe, *Interim CEO and Executive Director;* Stefani Roth, *Publisher;* Genny Ostertag, *Director, Content Acquisitions;* Julie Houtz, *Director, Book Editing & Production;* Joy Scott Ressler, *Editor;* Judi Connelly, *Senior Art Director;* Khanh Pham, *Graphic Designer;* Circle Graphics, *Typesetter;* Kelly Marshall, *Interim Manager, Production Services;* Shajuan Martin, *E-Publishing Specialist;* Tristan Coffelt, *Production Specialist.*

All web links in this book are correct as of the publication date below but may have become inactive or otherwise modified since that time. If you notice a deactivated or changed link, please e-mail books@ascd.org with the words "Link Update" in the subject line. In your message, please specify the web link, the book title, and the page number on which the link appears.

PAPERBACK ISBN: 978-1-4166-2790-6 ASCD product #118040
PDF E-BOOK ISBN: 978-1-4166-2792-0; see Books in Print for other formats.

Quantity discounts are available: e-mail programteam@ascd.org or call 800-933-2723, ext. 5773, or 703-575-5773. For desk copies, go to www.ascd.org/deskcopy.

ASCD Member Book No. FY19-9 (Aug. 2019 P). ASCD Member Books mail to Premium (P), Select (S), and Institutional Plus (I+) members on this schedule: Jan, PSI+; Feb, P; Apr, PSI+; May, P; Jul, PSI+; Aug, P; Sep, PSI+; Nov, PSI+; Dec, P. For current details on membership, see www.ascd.org/membership.

Library of Congress Cataloging-in-Publication Data

Names: Fullan, Michael, author. | Kirtman, Lyle.
Title: Coherent school leadership: forging clarity from complexity / Michael Fullan and Lyle Kirtman.
Description: Alexandria, VA: ASCD, 2019. | Includes bibliographical references and index.
Identifiers: LCCN 2019010118 (print) | LCCN 2019011098 (ebook) | ISBN 9781416627920 (Pdf) | ISBN 9781416627906 (pbk.: alk. paper)
Subjects: LCSH: Educational leadership—United States. | School management and organization—United States.
Classification: LCC LB2805 (ebook) | LCC LB2805 .F846 2019 (print) | DDC 371.2—dc23
LC record available at https://lccn.loc.gov/2019010118

27 26 25 24 23 22 21 20 19   1 2 3 4 5 6 7 8 9 10 11 12

Acknowledgments

I am blessed by co-learning with leaders around the world. Working and learning together is a never-ending proposition. I thank them all for this well-spring of knowledge.

To my immediate group: Claudia, Joanne Q., Santiago, Bill, MaryJean, Joanne M., Max, and Mag—small team, giant impact. Thanks for a lifetime of beautiful work.

—*Michael*

I would like to continue to thank my mother, who recently passed, for the foundation of values and commitment that continue to give me strength and guidance: my wife, Kathleen Keegan, for her patience, support, and guidance, personally and as a psychotherapist, in understanding the personal aspect of leadership for our clients; John Pierce, who is my thought partner and grounds me every day in the world of being a principal; Beth Saunders, who keeps me focused and my books on track to meet the needs of the reader; Stefan Kohler, who helped jump-start my career by believing in my work; and, finally, my son, Sean Kirtman, who keeps me current on leadership today in a global society.

— *Lyle*

Coherent School Leadership: Forging Clarity from Complexity

Michael Fullan & Lyle Kirtman

ORGANIZATIONAL COHERENCE AND LEADERSHIP COMPETENCIES

We've each spent more than three decades developing our own key theories of change—built from *practice*. For us, most insights come from close work through ongoing partnerships with those at all levels of the education system attempting to bring about positive change. Although a book that we wrote (Kirtman & Fullan, 2016) brought these ideas and insights about positive change management together, it didn't do so at as deep a level as this book will. In this book, we will turn our attention to what we didn't discuss previously— how to create coherence systems in today's fragmented and reactive world of education. Here we will discuss how to create coherence in both structure and behaviors and equip leaders to continuously improve their craft to provide the learning environment that students need to be successful in a fast-paced, dynamic world.

Fullan and Quinn

Fullan's latest consolidation of ideas can be found in *Coherence: The Right Drivers in Action for Schools, Districts, and Systems* (Fullan & Quinn, 2016). Based on close work with schools, districts, and states over the past decade, Fullan and Quinn concluded that organizations are most likely to suffer from fragmentation and overload when achieving focus was a problem. However, good focus is more than simple alignment; it must be supported by clarity and coherence. They defined coherence as "the shared depth of understanding about the nature of the work and how it impacts the results desired for student achievement" (p. 1). In other words, it is fully and solely *subjective.*

People often confuse alignment—making sure things are in a logical order—with coherence—the emotional state of grasping the clear meaning of a phenomenon.

To make it more challenging, coherence, in order to be effective, must be shared (i.e., the group must have a clear sense of where they want to go and are going). This is what makes it difficult to achieve. With all the commotion and churn, people have to obtain a good, subjective sense of their work life and organization and, to a large degree, they must share it. Fullan and Quinn, through their work with school districts and state systems, concluded that coherence consists of four interactive components—focusing direction, cultivating collaborative cultures, deepening learning, and securing accountability—and that leadership, which is at the core the framework, drills down and deals with the components individually and interactively (see Figure 1.1).

The first component of the Coherence Framework (the Framework)—focusing direction—is about vision and goals and consists of strategies to begin the coherence process. Developing the direction in practice requires purposefully cultivating collaborative cultures that begin to develop the essential capacities, at both the individual and collective levels, that will be needed going forward (the second component). The third component—deepening learning (the pedagogy or learning and teaching skills to engage and help students learn)—is at the heart of successful change.

They also found that traditional approaches to accountability (the fourth component), which emphasize tests and corrective action, were not effective at stimulating progress and that what worked was a focus on a few ambitious goals, collaborative work in relation to those goals, good engaging pedagogy, and accountability that developed within the group and, in turn, related to external accountability requirements.

FIGURE 1.1

The Coherence Framework

Finally, Fullan and Quinn found that coherence is not static—not some-thing that one can achieve and it's done—but is continuous. There are three things that make coherence continuous:

- People come and go in an organization and each personnel change rep-resents a coherence-making challenge and opportunity;
- The environment or context constantly changes in unpredictable ways—new technologies, population shifts, the economy, the future of jobs, climate, diversity, global and regional conflict, and the like; and, hopefully,
- People in an organization get new ideas—they innovate or engage in continuous improvement.

Overall, practitioners loved the Framework. It seemed to provide an answer to the problem of what to do with so many pieces that did not hang together. But, like most things that seem to be too good to be true, it was! Practitioners asked, "*How* do we get and keep coherence if we don't have it?" Although one could make some progress by working directly with the four components (the components) of the Framework, that was not enough. So, rather than focus solely on the components of coherence, Fullan and Quinn considered the *skills and competencies* that would be required to develop and maintain coherence. It was at this point that they decided to revisit Kirtman's 7 Competencies for Highly Effective Leaders and identify how to incorporate them into promoting organizational coherence and sustainable change.

Kirtman

The observation of highly effective leaders in action toward identifying the skills that were associated with their success led to the development of Kirtman's 7 Competencies for Highly Effective Leaders (the Competencies). The characteristics that the observed leaders shared were the ability to: challenge the status quo, build trust through clear communications and expectations, create a commonly owned plan for success, focus on team over self, maintain a high sense of urgency regarding change and sustainable results, commit to continuous improvement of self and the organization, and build external networks/partnerships—in effect, the competencies that constitute the leadership core of the Framework.

Fullan and Kirtman: A Marriage of Frameworks

The Competencies, as validated as they are, focused on the *individual leader*. There was a need for a solution that connected knowledge about individual leadership and organizational effectiveness. Hence, this book.

The Competencies do not "function" in the same manner—that is, some competencies "push" change and some "pull" change (see Figure 1.2).

FIGURE I.2

Competencies That Push Change and Competencies That Pull Change

Competencies That PUSH Change	Competencies That PULL Change
1. Challenges the status quo	3. Creates a commonly owned plan for success
2. Builds trust through clear communications and expectations	4. Focuses on team over self
5. Has a high sense of urgency for change and sustainable results	6. Is committed to continuous improvement of self and the organization
7. Builds external networks/partnerships	

Note

Competency 7—Builds external networks/partnerships—cannot cleanly be categorized as a "push" or "pull" competency. In some instances, a partnership may involve bringing an external party into the school or district toward benefiting the school or district and in other instances, a partnership may be beneficial for both the external organization and the district.

We can then explicitly link the components of the Framework and the Competencies (see Figure 1.3).

We know from our work on leading change that effective change requires that the components of the Framework be combined with leadership competencies that both "push" and "pull."

A SCHOOL IN TROUBLE

An urban school in the northeast was declared underperforming based on the statewide assessment. The school was not improving with the compliance requirements of the state. The teachers felt defeated and were embarrassed to be associated with the school—the lowest-performing school in the district. The superintendent suggested that the principal try a new approach to increase test scores. The principal used the Framework and focused on each of the components. The state provided guidance on setting clear direction for success based on data analysis. A focus on literacy was the core area for sustainable success.

FIGURE I.3

Linking the Components of the Framework and the Competencies

Coherence Framework Components	Competencies for Highly Effective Leaders
Focusing direction	Challenges the status quo
Cultivating collaborative cultures	Builds trust through clear communications and expectations; focuses on team over self; creates a commonly owned plan for success
Deepening learning	Builds external networks/partnerships
Securing accountability	Is committed to continuous improvement of self and the organization; has a high sense of urgency for change and sustainable results

Collaboration is where many districts go wrong. Many systems, ironically, mandate collaboration and adopt the strategy known as professional learning communities (PLCs). The Boston Consulting Group (BSG) conducted a study of teacher learning funded by the Gates Foundation and presented its findings in a report entitled *Teachers Know Best* (2014). The BSG found that although a high percentage of administrators valued PLCs as a strategy for improving schools, a much smaller percentage of teachers embraced PLCs. At the same time, when teachers were asked how they liked to learn, they named many of the putative elements of PLCs—working with and learning from other teachers, examining student work together, and so on. What was happening in the case at hand was that the district—the urban northeast district—had a history of teachers working in silos. In fact, teachers of grades that were performing at expected levels did not want to participate in whole-school meetings.

When the state mandated collaboration, the message fell on unreceptive ears. It was only when the principal received a coach who helped her develop a more sophisticated approach to collaboration that a breakthrough occurred. In effect, the intervention began to integrate the organizational solution—the Framework—with the competency skill set—the Competencies. Essentially the intervention enabled the focus on a "push" competency—*challenges the status quo* (Competency 1)—to begin the change process. This required working with the principal's leadership team on challenging the current practices in the school that were blocking success. The state's focus on compliance—you must collaborate—was given secondary status. The principal, in order to get the needed support of the leadership team, needed to immediately bring to the fore a "pull" competency—she chose *builds trust through clear communications and expectations* (Competency 2). The principal was transparent regarding the data, concerns, the areas on which she needed to work in order to be a better leader, and how she needed her leadership team to help her.

The next competency employed to "pull in" the rest of the school—*creates a commonly owned plan for success* (Competency 3)—serves to mobilize the whole staff. In this particular case, the plan was facilitated by the principal and the assistant principal with strong input from her leadership team and team of teachers. This planning process began the true work of collaboration (Component two) and coherence. This collaborative planning process and the honest and open conversations that took place across the school shifted the accountability (Component four) focus from one driven by the state to a plan in which all staff took ownership.

A SCHOOL NO LONGER IN TROUBLE

The school's student achievement increased by more than 50 percent in one year. The plan for success that was driven by the state was now owned by the whole school. The accountability (Component four) was intrinsically driven. Today, the principal would say that the reason her school succeeded was not about curriculum and instruction, and certainly not about compliance, but that it was about a "pull" competency—*focuses on team over self* (Competency 4). She now had a leadership team with which to share the leadership load. Yes, the deeper learning (Component three) was critical. However, it received traction for sustainable improvement through collaboration and teamwork.

As we've shown, the combination of the components of the Framework and the Competencies is the route to success. We recommend using the Framework as the organizing mechanism and the Competencies as a checklist and guide to developing skills of individuals and the team. (If you choose to use Kirtman's diagnostic instruments to build the Competencies, the components of the Framework must be the main organizer.)

The Organization of This Book

This book will go beyond typical leadership books that tell you what you need to put in place to enhance leadership. We will show you how to use specific competencies to drive coherence. We will provide examples that show how other leaders have successfully created coherence and used the leadership competencies to build sustainability. Although the examples provide models, you must extract what is relevant for your culture to begin this work. While our "how-to" steps will provide a platform, the order and magnitude of the steps will depend on your needs and your school community or district. The flow of the remaining chapters is as follows.

In **Chapter 2, The 7 Competencies for Highly Effective Leaders in Action**, we will show you how to use the Competencies in relation to the Framework. This chapter will also provide leadership principles of the 21st century that will help you apply the Competencies. For example, in the past, challenging the status quo (Competency 1) tended to be more top-down. In today's world of building capacity, the faculty/staff need to understand why the status quo is being challenged and be part of the continuous learning process.

Chapter 3, The Coherence Framework in Action, will explore what it would look like to have a truly coherent district. Would everyone be using all seven competencies? How does the behavior of the adults align with the behavior we expect from students? How does each component of the Framework look when it is in place? How does the district hire leaders who believe in and add to the skill base of coherence-making? Michael's international perspective allows us to bring international examples to our learning and application of best practices.

How can coherence stay on track despite systems overload, competing initiatives, day-to-day crises with student behavioral issues, adult personality conflicts, parent concerns, sudden budget cuts, school board personal agendas, tedious compliance requirements, and fragmentation that constantly destabilizes an organization? In **Chapter 4, Implementation and Execution Is Key**, we will discuss the often-neglected expansion of leadership to include management. As well, we will outline the steps to effectively implement change and improvement in a school or district to create sustainable results and show why effective implementation and often-neglected execution skills are key to forming the foundation for coherent leadership.

The concept of coherence is becoming more and more critical because the world is becoming more complex, and less and less predictable. This means that new leadership that can effectively work in the area of *coherence-making* is required. As mentioned previously, there are three things that make coherence continuous (people come and go in an organization, the environment or context changes in unpredictable ways, people in an organization get new ideas). In **Chapter 5, Leadership for the Future,** we will show that leaders of the future will need to become learners first, co-learners always, and learn to work interactively to forge the future through joint determination with those they lead. This chapter will consider forces that could both destabilize and integrate coherence in the future. We will take a world view of the forces that could destabilize education and the work of coherence—from the technology, political, pedagogy, and policy arenas—and that will help leaders stay ahead of the curve.

The net effect of this book will be to show how proven frameworks such as the Framework and the Competencies can help you cope with even the most complex scenarios. Our work comes from *practice*. The fact that practice is going to become even more unpredictable and constantly disrupted means that leaders will need grounded frameworks that can help them both influence and learn from the new world that is currently unfolding. Be ready for ever-greater challenges. Learners make the best leaders—this is the causal direction you should strive for.

THE 7 COMPETENCIES FOR HIGHLY EFFECTIVE LEADERS IN ACTION

The 7 Competencies for Highly Effective Leaders (the Competencies) are valuable, even when there are numerous hierarchical forms of leadership as has been the case over the past several decades. However, they have become even more effective in the new leadership paradigm that combines the Competencies and the Coherence Framework (the Framework). This new integrated model is based less on top-down vision and direct inspiration, and more on a type of leadership that requires enabling people to develop via lateral learning from others with leaders enabling networking, innovative solutions, and collective assessment of impact and ongoing learning. Fullan, Quinn, and McEachen (2018) have developed these ideas in relation to "deep learning," which mobilizes teachers who can develop students with global competencies who can thrive in complex times. The complexity of the times calls for a very different use of the Competencies, which are now desirable *and* essential.

In this chapter, we will provide an overview of the Competencies as they relate to each of the components of the Framework. In subsequent chapters, we will delve into the Competencies in action across the Framework.

Putting the Coherence Framework into Practice

The Framework provides us with four areas on which to focus coherence-making in a school or district that position the work and behaviors that are needed to provide sustainability in improving student achievement. The most common question we get about the Framework is, "We fully agree with the Framework, but *how* do we implement it, especially in complex times? In other words, what skills do I need to put the Framework into practice?" The short answer is that you need two things to put the Framework into practice:

- An awareness that the Framework is a dynamic framework within which the components constantly interact. The key is to understand each component and to foster interaction across them.
- An understanding that the Competencies must be developed.

However, it may not be clear how to connect the Competencies to coherence-making. What competency should you use to focus direction for the district? How does a leader apply the competency to the work with his leadership team, staff, board, and other key constituents?

This chapter will show you how to connect the Competencies to the components of the Framework, recognizing that each situation will have its particular requirements (e.g., some components of the Framework may require more attention than others). Before we show you how to connect the Competencies to the components of the Framework, we need to explore the leadership principles that guide us in leading in today's world of education. Following are some of the principles that you need to consider in today's education climate when using the Competencies for coherence-making.

Leading in the 21st Century

Simplexity

In *Coherence: The Right Drivers in Action for Schools, Districts, and Systems*, Fullan and Quinn (2016) discuss the concept of Simplexity. They state that complex situations need to be simplified to help focus the work of improving student achievement. The difficult, or complex, part of simplifying is ensuring that in doing so we are not losing the substance of the work and the inter-dependencies of issues required to achieve sustainable results. We need to simplify without oversimplifying. The more sophisticated aspects come into play as you put the components of the Framework and their interactions into practice. In short, the relatively simple part involves focusing on a small number of key factors, and the complex aspect consists of enabling these factors to synergize and otherwise interact.

Information *and* People Needed

In today's world of technology, information is easily available to everyone. A school district can potentially solve complex problems by creating a learning environment in which students and staff learn from one another. The power of an organization is in the people, not just in information. Schools need people to learn across departments, disciplines, and schools—vertically and horizontally.

Results Oriented Versus Task Focused

Leaders must be results oriented rather than task focused. Kirtman's research on leadership shows that school districts have become more task focused than process and results oriented, which has led to an overemphasis on compliance, too many meetings, slow decision making, and struggles with change. By contrast, sustained student achievement will require change processes that accomplish a lot in shorter periods of time and maximize results.

Work in Partnerships

A new approach to leadership and management is to work in partnership with groups considered to be outside the educational community that are actually inside the educational community (e.g., parents). Parents can be seen as being outside the school community and needing to "stay in their place." However, a principle of leadership today is to understand why and how parents need to be viewed as being inside the educational community. Parents working in concert with teachers on the educational process is key to success today.

Intrinsic Accountability

Today, innovation is part of our world as never before. There are countless ways to accomplish our goals. Finding new/innovative approaches to solve problems must be built on sound implementation strategies. Although new ideas are great, they don't count if they never see the light of day. A key principle from Kirtman's research and experience and Fullan's international viewpoint is the role of accountability. Intrinsic accountability creates a culture of continuous improvement. Creativity, risk taking, and innovation thrive in a culture of intrinsic accountability. The fourth component of the Framework—securing accountability—consists of developing internal (or intrinsic) accountability as the foundation for individual and collective responsibility. Intrinsic accountability occurs when the group doing the work develops transparent self-responsibility relative to the progress it is making toward reaching selected goals. As Richard Elmore (2004) stressed, no amount of external accountability will be effective in the absence of internal accountability.

As the group develops its internal accountability, they can more effectively engage the external accountability requirements, which include system standards, testing results, and related actions. In short, the group becomes a more effective partner in relation to overall accountability requirements and actions.

Shared Decision Making and Distributive Leadership

Shared decision making and distributive leadership (i.e., less focus on power) is very important under the new conditions that involve many more people in networked solutions. We need all talents in a district to help solve today's problems or meet challenges that we have not seen before. If we want people to engage and commit to the goals of a district, they need to be part of the decision-making process and have genuine opportunities to lead. The fear of leaders has been that they must maintain control when we need to shift to empowering all staff to enhance results for students.

Collaborative Cultures and School Improvement

David Brooks, in *Good Leaders Make Good Schools* (2018), speaks about the overwhelming success in improving schools with collaborative cultures. In a collaborative culture, both the superintendent and the school board, in setting the direction for the district, must collaborate with the administration. In effect, the Competencies guide us to a collaborative process wherein all parties involved understand why a coherent school district, not just a system of schools, is needed.

Simple Plans Versus Complex Strategic Plans

Many districts immediately turn to strategic planning to aid in coherence-making. While many elements of strategic planning can help set direction and potentially add to coherence-making, caution is warranted. It is important that everyone understand why it is important to change and what problems the district is trying to solve. Too many districts have developed strategic plans that are long and complex—and many of those districts are no more coherent that they were before they developed a strategic plan. Simple plans—or "skinny plans," as Fullan says—are a good application of Simplexity. Taking all the complex issues in a district and distilling them to a one- to three-page user-friendly document is critical for building coherence.

Connecting the Competencies to the Components of the Framework

It is important to realize that leadership is situational. Therefore, depending on the circumstances that occur and challenge a leader in coherence-making, there may be a number of competencies that can be called upon. What follows are the most likely ways that a leader can use the Competencies in the coherence-making process. We repeat our main message in this book: Coherence-making requires focusing on the components of the Framework while using the Competencies to navigate the Framework. Thus, we now turn to a detailed examination of the Competencies (see Figure 2.1) in relation to the components of the Framework.

FIGURE 2.1

Kirtman's 7 Competencies for Highly Effective Leaders and the Competency Subskills*

1. Challenges the status quo (Push)
   —Challenges common practices and traditions if they are blocking improvements
   —Is willing to take risks
   —Delegates compliance tasks to other staff
   —Does not let rules and regulations block results and slow down progress
   —Focuses on innovation to get results

2. Builds trust through clear communications and expectations (Push)
   —Is direct and honest about performance expectations
   —Follows through with actions on all commitments
   —Makes sure there is a clear understanding based on written and verbal communications
   —Is comfortable dealing with conflict

3. Creates a commonly owned plan for success (Pull)
   —Ensures that people buy into the plan
   —Creates written plans with input of stakeholders
   —Develops clear measurement for each goal in the plan
   —Monitors implementation of the plan
   —Adjusts the plan based on new data and communicates changes clearly
   —Creates short- and long-term plans

4. Focuses on team over self (Pull)
   —Seeks critical feedback
   —Supports the professional development of all staff
   —Commits to the ongoing development of a high-performance leadership team
   —Creates a team environment
   —Empowers staff to make decisions and get results
   —Hires the best people for the team

FIGURE 2.1

Kirtman's 7 Competencies for Highly Effective Leaders and the Competency Subskills*

5. Has a high sense of urgency for change and sustainable results (Push)
    —Is able to move initiatives ahead quickly
    —Can be very decisive
    —Uses instructional data to support needed change
    —Builds systemic strategies to ensure sustainability of change
    —Sets a clear direction for the organization
    —Is able to deal with and manage change effectively
6. Is committed to continuous improvement of self and the organization (Pull)
    —Has a high sense of curiosity for new ways to get results
    —Is willing to change current practices for themselves and others
    —Listens to all team members to change practices to obtain results
    —Takes responsibility for their actions (no excuses)
    —Has strong self-management and self-reflection skills
7. Builds external networks/partnerships
    —Uses technology to expand and manage a network of resources and people
    —Understands their role as being a part of a variety of external networks for change and improvement
    —Sees their role as a leader in a broad-based manner outside the work environment and community walls
    —Has a strong ability to engage people inside and outside in two-way partnerships

*The items under each competency are the subskills referred to in text.

Component One: Focusing Direction

This component involves:

- Purpose-driven mindset
- Goals that impact
- Clarity of strategy
- Change leadership

To begin to address this component of the Framework, the leader must identify where the strengths of the school exist and whether staff understand the direction of the school. In most cases, it will be necessary to use **Competency 1**—*Challenges the status quo,* which is a "push" competency. The use of this competency will challenge many of the practices and behaviors of those who are comfortable in the current system. At the same time, the key skill for the leader is how to challenge the status quo while beginning to build a partnership with those in the organization. In addition, the leader will need to use subskills to enhance his use of the competency to obtain maximum results. In effect, it will be necessary to combine and integrate "push" and "pull" competencies at the outset—a process that Fullan, in *Nuance: Why Some Leaders Succeed and Others Fail* (2019), called "joint determination."

> If a principal is trying to set direction and increase focus, there needs to be a challenge of current practices. If we consider the Competencies, the top-down approach to challenging the status quo will not be effective. The changes that the leader would like to see will not be owned by the staff. In addition, if there is an opportunity to challenge current practices, staff may surprise you and have their own effective challenges to the status quo. Paradoxically, the leader must understand the status quo and respect its qualities as she engages in identifying what might need changing. The **Competency 1 subskill** 'challenges common practices and traditions if they are blocking improvements' involves simultaneously being respectful of the

current practices and being clear on how those practices are blocking needed change and improvements.

Therefore, the principal needs to provide an exercise or a video that helps staff engage in a conversation of why the needs of students have changed. Staff need to explore the changing needs of students and society and how the role of the teacher needs to adjust. They need to understand why the practices of the past may not work today. Another approach to demonstrating how the needs of students are changing based on the demands of the world of work is to bring in alumni to speak to students and teachers. A select group of graduates who are in their mid-20s are now in the work world and can speak about how their education has helped them achieve. In addition, these graduates can be specific about how there are new skills that are key to success, which were not part of their K–12 education. In fact, you will find that these graduates might show how what are often referred to as "soft skills" are critical for their success. They might also point out that the 21st century skills were not part of their college education.

It is also important to connect with how the staff feel about how the school is working now. Are they frustrated, stressed, and having difficulty meeting the current demands that are coming from the district, state, and federal government? The frustration that most educators, especially teachers, are feeling creates a dissonance that can increase the openness to change—that is, the dissonance points out that staff, although hesitant to change, are willing to do so because the current environment is often not comfortable (for teachers) and is overly stressful.

The leader can co-create how the change process can work. Instead of forcing change, the case of urgency for change is created. The teachers are part of the change and will need guidance and coaching from their leaders in how to navigate the change in ways that increase success for students and minimizes stress for the adults.

Another Competency 1 subskill is 'is willing to take risks.' Regarding the change process, a teacher asked one of us, "Can we take risks in a safe way?" Overcoming fear of risk taking is critical to challenging the status quo. To help leaders and teachers take risks, it is important to plan out strategies for change, take small steps at first, and develop skills to effective risk taking.

The fear of risk taking can be mitigated through training on how to be a leader of change, not just a subject or sometimes the victim of change. Teachers will need to build their own skills to influence each other and the administration. The influence skill is key to effective change and is not dependent on positional authority. In a world where collaboration is key, the ability to influence is a core skill for expressing one's ideas and making effective change and improvement.

The additional Competency 1 can become relevant depending on the situation. For example, subskill 'delegates compliance tasks to other staff' will free up time for planning and managing the change process. The added time allows the leader to test ideas for change with key staff and builds a cadre of support for needed change and improvement. Subskill 'does not let rules and regulations block results and slow down progress' conveys that there must first be a focus on results and not on the rules that can slow down progress. This does not mean that breaking rules is paramount to challenging the status quo. Rather, it means that making sure that the rules and regulations are necessary to achieve the change and desired improvements. If the rules are important for results, they must be attended to with fidelity; if not, the ability to bend rules or meet minimum requirements could be key to challenging the status quo. As Kirtman states, "If the requirement is not key to results, however, then a *C* is more than enough, especially if it is accompanied by an *A* for teacher development and student learning" (Kirtman & Fullan, 2016, p. 69). This requires discussion with administrators and colleagues to minimize risk.

Lastly, **Competency 1 subskill** 'focuses on innovation to get results' is often key to challenging the status quo. Too often, innovation is stifled for compliance reasons. Innovation can be unbridled and not connected to improvement plans. Innovation for the sake of innovation is often distracting and can curtail coherence-making. If your current strategies for achieving needed change require changing current practices, innovation can be critical. However, it is very important to tie the innovation to how it will improve your results when past practices have stalled or failed.

•••••••

To employ Competency 1, you will need courage—courage to stay committed to effectively challenging others in line with your moral purpose—and a steadfast focus on improving the lives of your students!

Component Two: Cultivating Collaborative Cultures

This component involves:

- Culture of growth
- Learning leadership
- Capacity-building
- Collaborative work

If this component was the area of choice for improvement in your district, three competencies tend to be employed by leaders.

Competency 2

Competency 2—*Builds trust through clear communications and expectations*—is both a push and pull force. While the intent of this competency is to push people to a high level of performance and results, it is also effective in creating collaborative cultures—which, in turn, draws people in and supports them. Too often, leaders do not clearly communicate their expectations or provide direct feedback to staff to help them improve their practice.

The **Competency 2 subskill** 'is direct and honest about performance expectations' builds deeper trust than being too general and vague on improvements and only providing positive feedback. It is the balance of constructive critical feedback, along with positive comments, that helps staff improve their practice. The trust you earn is based on respect if the feedback is honest and not designed to just make people feel good.

By using Competency 2, the leader can begin to develop leadership capacity for administrators and teacher leaders. A leader needs to clarify the direction for the school and the expectations for growth of all staff—himself included. To employ the skills required for distributive leadership, the leader needs to talk about staff's strengths and areas for improvement in order to model the continuous improvement process. A number of leadership inventories can be used to assess your leadership style and your strengths and areas for growth. The principal, being the lead learner, can model the process of development and demonstrate that he is on the same level as the staff in the learning process—a key element in developing trust with your team. A leader who can show vulnerability is more powerful in collaborative cultures. Exploring structures such as staff meetings, performance evaluation processes, and decision-making models needs to occur to determine how they can be aligned with a true collaborative culture.

Another aspect of trust is delineated in **Competency 2 subskill** 'follows through with actions on all commitments.' Trust is so important; it is hard to gain and so easy to lose. Many see trust as the notion that you can be counted on to do what you say and meet deadlines and commitments. In other words, can I count on you? Making sure you have strong self-management systems and management skills that improve follow-through will help you build trust in your school or district.

The communication aspect of trust is further outlined in **Competency 2 subskill** 'makes sure there is a clear understanding based on written and verbal communications.' Too often people send out e-mails and documents with certain intent and do not personally connect with people to ensure understanding. We are so busy today we do not check for understanding, which erodes trust. It is important to understand how one builds trust with individuals and groups. The trust cycle, presented in Figure 2.2, is a very valuable tool that can be used when groups are beginning to exhibit conflict and the loss of trust.

FIGURE 2.2

The Trust Cycle

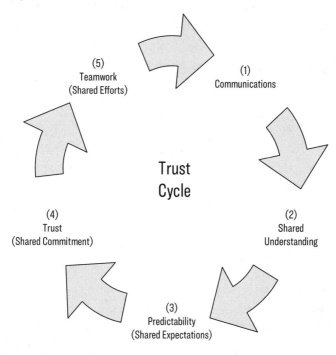

Source: Based on the work of Dr. Jerry Stinnett.

• • • • • • • • • • • • • • • • • •

THE TRUST CYCLE

The basis of the trust cycle is that people trust someone they find is predictable. Even Democrats and Republicans have been able to work together when the trust is evident—yielding consensus and positive results.

The trust cycle begins with *Communications*. One must clearly communicate her idea or point of view to her constituents.

The second stage of the cycle is *Shared Understanding*, which is where most leaders and groups lose trust. As noted throughout this book, people have very different problem-solving styles. They may also have values that result in polarization on a given issue. Making sure that what a leader has communicated is understood by the receiver is critical to building trust. Also, feedback about what is communicated can serve to clarify, refine, and add new ideas. Most leaders skip this stage in the cycle in their haste to rush to the fifth stage of the cycle—that is, they assume that teamwork can occur. The assumption that what is communicated is understood and that people can now work as a team to implement the new program or idea is often a factor in derailing a leader's initiative. As George Bernard Shaw said, "The single biggest problem in communication is the illusion that it has taken place" (Shaw, n.d.).

Many leaders do not want to take the time to make sure that people understand what has been communicated. They also hesitate to check for shared understanding because they believe that if people do not agree, they will sabotage the process of moving ahead. Leaders often do not understand that if trust is built properly, even disagreement will not prevent progress from occurring. However, not paying attention to the second stage of the cycle will result in many hours of wasted time because of misunderstandings and conflicts that will occur at later stages in the project.

Once the communications have occurred and there is a shared understanding, the dialog can move to the third stage of the cycle—*Predictability (Shared Expectations)*. At this stage, trust is built on a clear sense of predictable behavior. If this stage is bypassed, people will still predict behavior. However, the predictions will tend to be inaccurate and negative based on a lack of clear expectations, which will result in more mistrust based on perceived actions.

Stage four of the cycle is *Trust (Shared Commitment)*. This stage involves the distribution of responsibility and accountability to complete one's tasks or assignments. With shared commitment, people can count on one another to get the work done to reach the goal.

The commitment is strong at this point because trust is building on a sound base of understanding and expectations that are clear to all parties.

The fifth and final stage of the trust cycle—*Teamwork (Shared Efforts)*—is reached based on team goals developed in a safe and trusting environment. The team cannot just come about by throwing people into a room and giving them a project.

The realities presented in this chapter become insurmountable when the trust is absent and people talk behind each other's backs and work against the goal for personal reasons (Kirtman, 2014). (The trust cycle is further explained in *Leadership and Teams: The Missing Piece of the Educational Reform Puzzle* [Kirtman, 2014].)

•••••••••••••••••••••••

The final **Competency 2 subskill** is 'is comfortable dealing with conflict.' To gain trust, leaders must be vulnerable and able to effectively hear and value critical feedback and be comfortable working through conflict. Too often, people avoid conflict and choose simple answers to complex problems. Avoiding conflict has a negative effect on your credibility as a leader. Staff will trust you if you lean into conflict and stay focused on what is best for students and work collaboratively toward making sound decisions.

While there are issues such as safety that may require fast action and a top-down urgent style of decision making, an effective, collaborative school or district can make many decisions based on consensus. There are models for consensus decision making that can simultaneously be efficient and result in buy-in. Figure 2.3 illustrates the different decision-making styles that we see throughout districts.

Competency 4

If cultivating collaborative cultures was the area of choice for improvement in your district, the second competency that a leader would employ is (pull) Competency 4—*Focuses on team over self.*

FIGURE 2.3

Decision-Making Styles

Role	Decision-Making Styles				
	1	2	3	4	5
Leader	Decides	Proposes	Listens	Co-Designs	Gives team responsibility
Team	Implements	Provides Input	Consults	Co-Designs	Works with a framework

Style 1: Leader announces decision to the team and the team implements.

Style 2: Leader has formulated a proposal about the best alternative for the decision that must be made. The leader seeks input from the team to determine if the team can persuade her to rethink her decision before implementation.

Style 3: Leader has a decision to make and does not have an opinion about the best alternative. The leader consults with the team before choosing the best alternative.

Style 4: Leader and the team co-design the decision and the implementation process.

Style 5: Leader will serve as a resource to the team and may provide parameters for decision making. The team will make a decision without the involvement of the leader (unless needed). The leader will support the decision of the team and will ensure that the team and the leader work together.

Teaching is often a lonely position and, in many districts, schools operate in a silo. Employing this competency entails explaining what a highly functioning team looks like. Teaching leaders about how to develop a team rather than a group of staff is core to collaboration.

Once new expectations are clear and the direction is effectively communicated, your leadership team needs to learn how to develop effective teams and build teams across your school or district. For example, a professional learning community (PLC) needs to learn how to be an effective team to be able to maximize learning for students. Effective teams frequently work across disciplines and rely on each other to obtain results. Often trust is the first area for focus. Trust issues must be surfaced honestly and discussed before a team can move toward common purpose and actions. As with all of the Competencies, trust building is a *process*. People develop trust as a result of new experiences that demonstrate trust in action. For example, if a leader espouses a climate of risk taking (i.e., it is okay to make mistakes as long as you learn from them), she will have to model that behavior in her own work and support it in the action of others.

To be able to build trust, leadership teams (and even PLCs) need to be coached on how to have direct conversations. Kirtman's research on high-performing leaders indicates that most educators avoid having "difficult conversations" and struggle with giving and receiving constructive criticism. A team needs to be able to talk about issues honestly and to admit what they could have done differently to get better results. (Competency 2 is a "push" competency because it moves people out of their comfort zones into conversations that are truly honest and open.) The best teams seek critical feedback (**a Competency 4 subskill**). Too often, teams believe they are respected without seeking out feedback to confirm their assumptions.

To develop and maintain effective teams, the other **Competency 4 subskills** must be applied. The team needs to identify its professional development plan, which could involve skill building on instructional issues or on the ability to manage conflict. The ultimate sign of a strong team is the ability of the leader to trust, empower, and support team members to make decisions and get results. This "letting go" behavior frees up the leader's time for strategic issues and builds capacity to increase effectiveness in a school or district.

Another aspect of building a team and maintaining coherence is in hiring the best people. Too often, transitions in leadership break apart teams and ultimately lose momentum on coherence making. The Competencies should be used in the hiring process to maintain the team's effectiveness. Key questions on each competency can be created and added to the hiring process.

Competency 3

The third competency associated with cultivating collaborative cultures is (pull) Competency 3—*Creates a commonly owned plan for success*. The plan must be based on the content of the work in the school and include how the staff will work together. Remember: All plans should be "skinny plans," simple to digest, and should focus direction. (In Chapter 4, we will outline how a new approach to establishing group and team norms can be part of your school plan.)

The Competency 3 subskills are key to collaboration in the planning and implementation process. It is important to get input early from all constituents in your planning efforts. You will need them to support you through the action stage and their early involvement will gain their ownership. Getting them to buy into the plan comes from their involvement. It is important to show some change of plans or a specific strategy that came from each group's input.

A plan must have clear measurements. This is a difficult aspect of many planning processes. Too many plans have general goals without clear measurements. Other plans have measurements that are too narrow. Many leaders are concerned that measurements can be used against them in a punitive manner. However, how will you know you are successful if no one is clear on the outcome? SMART—specific, measurable, attainable, relevant, and time-bound—goals are used in many districts to make sure there is a measurable outcome. Unfortunately, SMART goals in a punitive environment (i.e., an environment without trust and collaboration) may become too narrow or so easy to reach that they become meaningless. We recommend identifying measurements as indicators of success. This will allow a goal to have one to three indicators. If an indicator is not reached, it does not mean failure. Failure to reach an indicator warrants exploring why and adjusting future plans—a constructive way to employ measurements without the potential of creating a punitive culture of blame that exists in many organizations.

The ability to monitor and adjust plans is critical to a collaborative environment. The term "planning" implies that strategies may change based on implementation challenges. The monitoring should be goal-oriented and connected to the indicators of success. It is not advisable to monitor every strategy and action, as that will result in too much compliance, paperwork, and too much focus on the tasks. Outcomes, not tasks, should be monitored. Monitoring and adjusting plans support the focus on the "why" and the "what," but not on the "how" of work in schools. The "how" should be up to the practitioners.

Communication of plans and adjustments of plans to the whole school or district community supports a collaborative culture. The community owns the plan and needs to help revise, update, and help with the implementation. Communication creates a feeling of transparency, which in turn builds trust.

The final **Competency 3 subskill** is 'creates short- and long-term plans.' Fullan, who emphasizes skinny plans, recommends 30-day short-term plans (as faster planning cycles often result in improved results). However, there still is a need for long-term plans, which can have short-term cycles of action.

Component Three: Deepening Learning

This component involves:

- Clarity of learning goals
- Precision in pedagogy
- Shifting practices through capacity-building

Depending on the level of instructional expertise and skill and the culture's openness to change, although many, if not all, of the competencies can be used in this core work of schools, **Competency 7**—*Builds external networks/partnerships*—may be most effective.

The opportunity to build networks/partnerships in education is greater today than in the past. Leaders must extend their learning out to other schools in a district and to other communities in their state both nationally and internationally. Capabilities for deepening learning can be assessed based on internal resources and the expertise of statewide associations and networks. The expertise may include specific strategies for curriculum and potential human resources personnel to share experiences and expertise with your district. The Internet and social media can, for very little cost, enhance and deepen learning:

> One of us set up a video conference on project-based learning (PBL) in Connecticut, Massachusetts, and California to facilitate the exchange of best practice in enhancing curriculum on PBL. As a result,

the districts in Connecticut and Massachusetts, which were separately exploring enhancing curriculum on PBL, were able to learn from the Napa School District—which was at the center of the PBL movement.

While using this leadership principle for the 21st century, it is wise to develop a partnership with parents to deepen learning. While in some communities it may be challenging to secure the commitment of the parents, it is essential that parents understand and be supported in their role. In many urban districts, it may be difficult to get working parents to make a time commitment, and in more affluent districts, parents may be too controlling and overly involved. No matter the situation, leaders need to adopt the best practices of other districts to make parents partners in deepening learning—which may also involve making parents a part of the decision-making process:

> Recently, a district was receiving a range of complaints about social media's negative effect on learning due to its distractive nature. The district, which had previously asked parents to let the schools manage the problem, is changing its tune. Leaders asked an active parent to be part of a discussion with the administration about the issues with social media. The parent was surprised that the administration was open to her opinion. The district used some of the parent's ideas to manage social media and maintain the focus on learning. The parent, who had publicly accused the district of pushing parents out and not handling social media properly, is now a public supporter of the administration.

The Competency 7 subskills can broaden and enhance deeper learning. The vast number of resources nationally available on the Internet allows us to learn from districts in every area of learning. If one understands and accepts that there is someone out there who has an approach for your school on math, writing, or reading that will help your students, the options for networking are extraordinary. Taking the time to reach out will save you from having to create everything yourself. You can always adapt any approach to meet your school's needs. Instructional leadership must be thought of as both an inward and outward practice—that is, the best leaders are networkers and are always learning from people both within the field of education and from outside resources. Michael has the opportunity to learn from the world stage on how to effectively increase success for students. Lyle frequently states that every challenge he sees in a district has a corresponding solution in another. Using technology, tapping into multiple networks of support, and engaging your parents and community in the learning process will deepen learning for your students and constituents. It is important to learn one key aspect of networking and partnership: Truly successful external collaborations are two-way. It is important to learn about other's needs, to give before you take. Networks grow from relationships and stall when people are solely trying to benefit from others.

Component Four: Securing Accountability

This component involves:

- Internal and external accountability

If this component was the area of choice for improvement in your district, two competencies tend to be employed by leaders.

Competency 6

Based on the leadership principles, we need to develop an intrinsic drive in all leaders and staff to grow. Using (pull) Competency 6—*Is committed to continuous improvement of self and the organization*—is core to the switch in focus from external to internal accountability. Per Fullan and Quinn (2016), if you build the intrinsic internal drive for continuous improvement, the external accountability will improve. This competency must also be modeled by the leader. If the leader talks about his internal growth and development with his team, he makes it safe for staff to acknowledge that there are areas for improvement. In a true collaborative culture, colleagues can serve as resources for one another for growth. The accountability comes from applying the growth and development to improving their practice and increasing student success. Using data and the clarity on the results one is trying to achieve is paramount to a continuous improvement culture. If a teacher agrees that they have certain strengths in motivating students but have a difficult time in organizing the classroom to maximum time for results, that is a strength and not a weakness. The strength is being self-aware and committed to improve. If an outside evaluator tells you to improve, it is less effective and motivating than if you realize it yourself and commit to improving your practice.

Another step that should be taken to set up a continuous improvement competency that will secure accountability is to alter the performance evaluation process so that it is staff-driven and connected to measurements of results for students. This means teachers, unless they are fearful of the evaluation process, will be able to increase their focus on improving results for students. A teacher or administrator who does not feel attacked or judged will be much more motivated to improve. Likewise, if a teacher or administrator sees the evaluation process as a way to enhance their school's ability to help students achieve rather than as a compliance task they have to survive, the school culture for collaboration and results will improve.

We encourage you and your team to talk about failures and approaches that have not worked. The fear of failure in schools often blocks innovation and creativity. The admission of failure without repercussion can free staff to experiment and try new approaches. The compliance and outside evaluation of education has curtailed our ability to provide the innovation and creative environment we need for student learning. Coherence is not helping students prepare for a world of innovation, creativity, and teamwork by focusing on compliance and individual performance.

The Competency 6 subskills will help you develop and manage your continuous improvement effort. Curiosity is essential for continuous improvement. The desire to learn and hear new ideas and to determine how they can help you grow is very important. Once someone accepts that learning is an internal process not driven from external people telling them what to do and not just doing what they are told, people become empowered. Openness to changing current practices and learning from others is an attitude shift. Phrases such as "We tried that before," "This will not work," "Our district is different than yours and it will never work in our community" stifle learning and growth. Although all new ideas may not work, we must be open to listen to see if a new idea or approach helps us rethink our practice. Being reflective is the key to continuous improvement:

> Recently, one of us was involved in a teacher leader program in a suburban district. The teachers had the opportunity to complete a leadership assessment and reflect on what they are learning about themselves. One teacher reflected on her experience by saying that she wished she had the opportunity to look at her personal leadership style in her first year of teaching. She said that the first year was filled with an overwhelming number of new things that she had to learn and understand. She went on to say that it would have helped if she knew who she was and how to cope with the enormous number of requirements that were coming at her all at once.

The internal self-knowledge would have given her more balance and perspective. The power of self-reflection and insights teaches us more than we know. Continuous learning requires taking responsibility for our actions and not blaming others or using excuses. It requires us to manage our time and our lives without expecting others to take care of us.

Competency 5

While Competency 6 is important to switch from external accountability to intrinsic accountability for sustainable improvement, Competency 5—*Has a high sense of urgency for change and sustainable results*—is also needed. Having a high sense of urgency for results in improving student achievement must be the focus of your internal improvement process. The method of reflection in education has been more focused on empowerment without urgency for results for students. Reflection was an internal self-growth process. We believe reflection needs to be connected to a proactive, not reactive, sense of urgency. The frenetic reactive environments in education (which we will explore in Chapter 4) have not connected results to continuous improvement. A superintendent once said to one of us that lower-performing districts have a sense of urgency that is driven by the state or federal government as opposed to being internally driven. The sense of urgency of higher-performing districts, which also need to improve, is usually internally driven. The superintendent went on to say that lower-performing districts are required to change, while higher-performing districts need to be inspired to change.

The Competency 5 subskills play an important role. Sense of urgency involves moving to results faster with less focus on process and task completion. This can involve **Competency 5 subskill** 'is able to move initiatives ahead quickly.' One caution that Kirtman identifies is that fragmented initiatives can often decrease results and, as Fullan states, undermine coherence. Districts might consider, instead of using the word "initiatives," using Kirtman's substitute phrase "high-impact strategies"—which will mean that new innovation only occurs when current strategies or efforts are not working, thus decreasing the "initiative de jour" mentality and fatigue that is often created in the federal government, states, and districts. Teachers are not very excited to each year hear about the new initiatives in their district.

The ability of leaders to be decisive and act rather than delay action for fear of failure is key to achieving results for students and meeting the external test requirements nationally. Using instructional data to support needed change is key to successfully increasing the sense of urgency for strategic action. Data are important to show urgency and to determine whether actions are achieving the needed impact for student success. Data also help leaders in the continuous improvement process to provide feedback on how one can improve their practice.

A sense of urgency for sustainable results requires faster action. However, if plans and strategies are not systemic, we can experience short-term results that can plateau, which may halt districtwide improvement or even cause student achievement to regress. If you are a short-term action person, while we applaud your courage to act, we implore you to think more "big picture" for greater impact of improvement that reaches other schools and more students and that can last over time.

A sense of urgency for results provides direction and focus for self-improvement. Without clear direction, self-improvement, though it can be satisfying, may not move the needle ahead for students. The final **Competency 5**

subskill is 'is able to deal with and manage change effectively.' A sense of urgency forces all of us to change. The change process needs to be part of plans for improvement to show the understanding and commitment to support staff throughout the change process. The fear of change must be taken seriously. The self-reflection process for continuous improvement should include work and training for everyone on how they adapt to change.

••••••

To make the work manageable, it is important that leaders consider with staff all of the components of the Framework to get an overview of where their strengths and weaknesses might lie. The organization could then choose an area of coherence on which to improve and employ the proper competencies to drive the improvement. Balance the push and pull competencies based on the culture of your school or district. Talk as a team about your change and leadership work and be a learning organization as you enhance your leadership craft.

We are now in a position to show you the Framework in action. Chapter 3 begins by answering the question, "What do the Competencies look like in practice in relation to the Framework?"

THE COHERENCE FRAMEWORK IN ACTION

For at least the past two decades, the Fullan team has worked with school districts around the world in multiple capacities—research, consultancy and development, and filming—and this work led to the development of the Framework. In this chapter we draw on the team's experiences in Ontario (Canada), California, Massachusetts, and London.

No school or district that has been successful follows the Framework in a step-by-step manner. Successful change does not come from following a step-by-step manual. We know that the successful (which we'll soon define) districts (which comprised as few as four schools to as many as 200+ schools) followed similar paths, focused on a small number of key elements, were comprehensive and relentless in the pursuit of transformation, and had a good degree of longevity of success (a minimum of 10 years). Without referring to the Competencies by name, the leaders in all the districts were masters of the Competencies. Figure 3.1 details the locations, names, and number of schools in the districts. Although the demographics of the districts or schools are not noted, the vast majority of the sample is based in diverse, poor, immigrant communities.

FIGURE 3.1

Districts by Location and Number of Schools

Location	District	Number of Schools
Ontario	Ottawa Catholic School Board	83
	York Region District School Board	220
California	Garden Grove Unified School District	70
	Long Beach School District	91
	Sanger Unified School District	20
	Whittier Union High School District	5
Massachusetts	Quaboag Regional School District	4
London	London Borough of Hackney	97
	London Borough of Tower Hamlets	73

How does one define success in relation to district performance? One of the core principles in our system work is that schools and districts must focus on causal pathways to measurable outcomes. They must be able to explain how they got results or failed to do so. We do this not to please the state accountability system (although it serves that purpose), but rather so that the organization can understand progress and how to get more of it. We do not focus on tests—literacy, numeracy, high school graduation, and the like—although the measures in all cases include these; we also value engagement, satisfaction, well-being, and the 6 Cs of global learning—character education, citizenship, communication, critical thinking and problem solving, collaboration, and creativity and imagination. It is the case that not all these measures are available, but many are being developed by us and by others.

In the rest of this chapter, we will start with success or outcomes and then double back to trace the factors that led to success. In the final section of the chapter, we will examine leadership in the context of systemwide success.

Districtwide Success

We will in this section focus on the *outcomes* of various districts because we first want to establish that the cases represent *successful leadership in action.*

OTTAWA CATHOLIC SCHOOL BOARD

In the Ottawa Catholic School Board, from 2005 to 2009, the district improved steadily in all six performance scores—proficiency in reading, writing, and math for 3rd and 6th grades—assessed by the province. On four of these measures (writing and math for grades 3 and 6), there was an increase in the baseline from 60 percent to 75 percent, and slightly lower increases in 3rd and 6th grade reading. The district has further increased its gains from 2010 to 2018, including taking on deep learning districtwide (see Fullan, Quinn, & McEachen, 2018).

YORK REGION DISTRICT SCHOOL BOARD

York Region District School Board, a highly diverse urban school district just north of Toronto, has experienced rapid growth over the past 18 years—and now, with some 220 schools, is still expanding. We have worked with the district and its superintendent, Bill Hogarth, since 1999. York Region's primary focus was on low-performing schools. In 2006, it identified six secondary schools and 17 low-performing elementary schools that needed improvement. In many of the schools, we saw huge gains in literacy over a three-year period—from 65 to more than 80 percent in some schools. In 2005, there was a gain of 5 percent in literacy across a total of 140 elementary schools.

Overall, from 1999 to 2009, this large, growing, diverse school district improved in just about every dimension (see Fullan, 2010, Fullan & Quinn, 2016). Since 2010, the district has had three directors and a number of problems, but that is another story. We can learn a great deal from its 11 years of success, and from its recent troubles (which we won't detail, as it would take us away from the main themes of this chapter).

QUABOAG REGIONAL SCHOOL DISTRICT

In Quaboag Regional School District, the growth in student achievement has been significant. In 2009, the district was rated underperforming by the state. New superintendent Brett Kustigian led the district from underperformance to being recognized for excellence. His strategy for success challenged the status quo by giving students the option of taking AP classes or honors classes. He eliminated the college-prep track (since the results were stagnant). While in 2010 there were four AP classes, there are now 13 AP classes. In 2013, 2015, 2017, and 2018, *US News and World Report* cited the high school for excellence and improvement in student achievement. Brett believes the focus on AP classes raised the level of performance for all students.

LONG BEACH SCHOOL DISTRICT, GARDEN GROVE UNIFIED SCHOOL DISTRICT, AND SANGER UNIFIED SCHOOL DISTRICT

Let's move to California. Long Beach, Garden Grove, and Sanger are long-standing successes and show similar cumulative and long-term results.

Long Beach has demonstrated increasingly strong performance and depth since the mid-90s under the leadership of superintendent Carl Cohn (1992–2002) and his deputy superintendent Chris Steinhauser (2002–present). Since 1992, literacy rates increased steadily, high school dropout rates decreased by two-thirds and, most noteworthy (as we shall see in the next section), Long Beach's capacity for continuing and deepening learning has strengthened districtwide.

The success experienced by Garden Grove is almost parallel to that experienced by Long Beach. Garden Grove flourished under the leadership of superintendent Laura Schwalm (2000–2013) and current superintendent Gabriela Mafi (who previously served as Schwalm's deputy). In 2004, the graduation rate in Garden Grove was 24 percent below the state average, with reading and math scores in the lowest percentiles. By 2015, scores in all subjects assessed exceeded the state average. Students in the district outperform their higher-performing urban peers.

Sanger is a small district comprising 20 schools. In 1999, the local teacher's union announced on a billboard, "Welcome to the home of 400 unhappy teachers!" In 2004, Sanger was placed on California's "program improvement list" as one the lowest-performing districts in the state. Marc Johnson was appointed superintendent in 2004 and promptly began the transformation process. In less than a decade, Sanger's scores exceed the state average on the Academic Performance Index. A union leader stated, "There is not a principal in this town that I would not work for" (David & Talbert, 2013, p. 3). As of 2018, Sanger continues to be a high-performing district.

WHITTIER UNION HIGH SCHOOL DISTRICT

Whittier Union High School District, a high-poverty district with three high schools (and partnership with its feeder elementary schools), was on the right track when superintendent Sandy Thorstenson began the development process in 2003. The district has shown improvement in student performance every year at each of its three schools on multiple indicators over the past 15 years—all the more remarkable in light of the fact that its poverty rates have climbed over this period (Fullan & Quinn, 2016).

LONDON BOROUGHS OF HACKNEY AND TOWER HAMLETS

Hackney and Tower Hamlets are two high-poverty London borough districts. Over the period of a decade (2004–2014), each district went from being well below England's national average on academic indicators of performance to equal to or above the national average. For example, in 2004, Tower Hamlets was some 14 percent below England's national average in secondary advance course achievement. By 2011, this gap of 14 percent was eliminated with Tower Hamlets reaching the national average. In national tests for English, math, and science for 11-year-olds, the considerable gap that in 1998 existed between the two boroughs and the country average was effectively closed by 2004. Both boroughs have continued to improve in the past decade (see Fullan & Boyle, 2014).

In sum, we have nine districts—nearly all with schools with diverse, high-poverty populations—in three countries that beat the odds and demonstrated continuous improvement, most of them for a decade or more. The key question now is, do these success stories have anything in common when it comes to strategies for change and leadership?

Note

For further detail on the districts, see Fullan, 2010 (Ottawa Catholic School Board and Long Beach School District), Fullan and Quinn, 2016 (York Region District School Board, Garden Grove Unified School District, Sanger Unified School District, London Borough of Hackney, and London Borough of Tower Hamlets), and Fullan and Quinn, 2016 and Fullan, 2017 (Sanger Unified School District and Whittier Union High School District).

The Framework and the Competencies and Districtwide Success

In many ways, the idea of coherence and the identification of competencies that each of us have identified and written books about have been derived from the successful examples of the past 20 years (such as the nine districts whose successes we previously outlined). In other words, the leaders in those cases did not have such frameworks in mind and then applied them. Researchers like us are really more interested in applied solutions so that we can clarify, develop, condense, and disseminate it to others for their own edification and application. In fact, even if we get it right and formulate clear lessons, we do not advocate that you use our frameworks in a formulaic manner. The fundamental issue in organizational change is that each situation to a certain degree is different. Starting points, history, and cultures are different. Our frameworks are not ideas to be applied in a step-by-step fashion, but rather frames for thinking and action. Two guidelines in particular are worth emphasizing:

- The main task is to change *the culture of the district*.
- Each situation has its own *distinct culture*. That is, any strategy must be shaped with the local culture as part and parcel of the solution.

Nonetheless, we would claim that the districts represent sustained attention to the frameworks presented in this book—the Coherence Framework (the Framework) and the 7 Competencies for Highly Effective Leaders (the Competencies). Although different terms may be used here and there, the concepts are essentially the same. We will use the Framework to organize this section, encompassing the Competencies as we go.

When you move to action, it is misleading to think of the Framework as four different pieces. The Framework as a whole is analogous to a healthy heart: there are four chambers with blood flowing in and out of each chamber. If any chamber is weak, you become ill or die. The same applies to the Framework and systems: if any one of the components—focusing direction, cultivating collaborative cultures, deepening learning, securing accountability—fails, the organization as a whole falters. In short, leaders must take into account all of the components of the Framework as they proceed with coherence-making.

We will pair the first two components—focusing direction and cultivating collaborative cultures—because they need to be seamless and indeed feed on each other interactively, and then we will examine the third and fourth components—deepening learning and securing accountability—as a pair.

Focusing Direction and Cultivating Collaborative Cultures

Focusing direction. Here is what Laura Schwalm, former superintendent of Garden Grove Unified School District, had to say about focusing direction:

"You need to be preoccupied with focus: a state or condition permitting clear perception or understanding; to direct your attention to something specific; a main purpose or interest. With so many issues that feel urgent, the necessity to focus is often overwhelmed by the number and magnitude of the problems faced by the system leader. You need 'one main thing' or central improvement strategy that consists of the leader's nonnegotiable view of what, over time, will have the greatest impact on improving the systems performance for children" (Fullan & Quinn, 2016, pp. 8–9).

In York Region District School Board, superintendent Bill Hogarth stunned the system in 1999 at the beginning of his tenure when he announced that all students in the district should be reading by the end of 1st grade. He and his colleagues then developed a clearly articulated vision and commitment to literacy, including the development of collaborative teams at both the school and district levels that was continually communicated in the districts.

Similarly, in London Borough of Hackney, leaders promulgated "an up-front, nonnegotiable goal and expectations that all kids will learn" and committed to a districtwide strategy that built capacity in each school and developed "focused collaboration across all primary and all secondary schools" (Fullan & Quinn, 2016, pp. 199–200).

In the same vein, we see the key competencies embedded in the actions. Focusing direction is expressed in specific nonnegotiable terms. It challenges the status quo (Competency 1) unequivocally.

Cultivating collaborative cultures. There is no doubt where the leaders stand relative to the impact on learning for all students, particularly for students not doing well. These leaders use transparent evidence of existing student achievement as the starting point. At the same time, these systems do not make the mistake of imposing high expectations, as if moral purpose could carry the day by itself, as Sanger has as one of its three core principles, "Hope is not a strategy." All of these districts did what Kirtman identified as competencies: built trust though clear communication and expectations (Competency 2) and created a commonly owned plan for success (Competency 3).

There are several critical subskills associated with these actions. Rather than blame schools for existing low performance, these systems work to support educators to become part of the solution. They invest in the development of the capacity of existing staff, and they use all hiring opportunities to reinforce the new direction. Trish Okoruwa, director of London Borough of Hackney, had this to say about what it was like when she was a school head:

"There wasn't any relationship to the system in those days, and there was no guidance. We had a different slogan every year and a folder would come out with no plan as to how you would actually get there" (Fullan, 2013, p. 19).

Later, when Okoruwa was deputy director and then director, she stressed that there was no question that the system leadership was being pushy, but there was "facilitation to have a dialogue about what it would look like without the blame culture attached to it" (Fullan, 2013, p. 19).

In all of the case examples referred to in this chapter, the systems developed leaders, from top to bottom, who "participate as learners" with others in building a commonly owned and specific plan of action. Trish Okoruwa talks about her dual strategy of "predict and prevent" and "find and fix." Hackney certainly is preoccupied with the moral purpose and ambition of the system, but what is more insightful for our purposes is how cultures shape and operate on a day-to-day basis. As Okoruwa describes it:

"Describing the *how* is the closest thing to be able to describe the culture and expectations within the organization. Hence, it is valuable for shaping the culture internally and equally valuable for communicating our approach externally in terms of a brand or value proposition. Talking about how we do things and why our way is better is communicated and built at every level of the organization" (Fullan, 2013, p. 105).

Quaboag Regional School District superintendent Brett Kustigian stated to Lyle:

"Our focus on AP and honors raised expectations for all students. In many rural communities, we do not accept the lack of resources as an excuse for not being excellent. Our approach raised expectations for all students, staff, faculty, administrators, and the community" (personal communication, 2018).

In order to raise expectations across the board, Quaboag needed to reach out and build networks and partnerships to supplement the lack of resources available. Quaboag partnered with Massachusetts Math and Science Initiatives and Jobs for the Future to broaden their resource base.

We can benefit from reaching out to our colleagues, gain new approaches from the successes and mistakes of others, and even learn from people outside education to save time and enhance our success. Brett networks every day as a matter of course. He has a full-time grant writer on staff (which you rarely see in small rural communities). He knows that he must challenge the status quo and reach out nationally for any funding opportunities.

Our key message here is that these systems manage to combine very high, no-nonsense expectations for student learning with a no-blame culture and processes that develop capacity, commitment, and ownership in the enterprise as a whole. The Framework and the Competencies reinforce each other to help systems get off to a strong new start in systems of transformation.

Deepening Learning and Securing Accountability

Deepening learning. Deepening learning, or learning more basically, is a bit tricky to deal with because for us it is undergoing, and should undergo, a transition. One aspect of success is doing well in the basics—literacy, numeracy, high school graduation rates. Another aspect of success is doing well in what we refer to as the global competencies—character education, citizenship, communication, critical thinking and problem solving, collaboration, creativity and imagination. We will leave this distinction aside for the moment until we establish some basic points. Let's start with learning.

As strange as it may sound, teaching and learning have, until recently, neglected pedagogy. Policymakers and many educators refer to standards, tests, and curriculum, but not so much the nature of teaching and learning. Several scholars have written whole books on the black box of implementation—neglect of actual practice. When you combine the Framework and the Competencies, it is impossible to neglect learning (and, as we will see, matters of accountability).

With explicit, specific high expectations (focused direction) and having cultivated a collaborative culture, you inevitably face pedagogy and its impact. Fullan and his colleague Andy Hargreaves (Hargreaves & Fullan, 2012) have pinpointed what effective collaboration looks like and how crucial it is to success. They have critiqued superficial collaboration where educators get together but do not get down to specifics or fail to act or follow through. In *Professional Capital: Transforming Teaching in Every School*, Fullan and Hargreaves showed that effectiveness of teaching must combine individual, social, and decisional capital—that is, quality of the individual, quality of the group, and quality of data–informed decisions, respectively (Hargreaves & Fullan, 2012). *Coherence: The Right Drivers in Action for Schools, Districts, and Systems* (Fullan & Quinn, 2016) spells out what collaborative culture looks like in practice. In a large-scale study, Hargreaves and colleague Michael O'Connor (2018) identify "collaborative professionalism" in terms of 10 tenets. One key insight in all of this work is that autonomy is not isolation, and professionalism must combine and treat autonomy and collaboration as equally crucial and as operating as a two-way street. As we shift our attention to deepening learning—component three—we can see how the coherence and competency integration makes the focus on learning inevitable. Coherence says you must carry over nonnegotiable high learning expectations and purposeful collaboration into improving teaching and learning practices for all.

We can see this inevitability and integration in what is called in one of the California districts we examined "the Garden Grove way," the four elements of which are as follows:

- Continuous improvement of instructional quality and spreading the best instructional practices and ideas to achieve learning goals across the system. Core strategies were identified and consistent support is provided to build expertise at all levels.
- Building teacher capacity is seen as the route to improvement (as Schwalm says, "You are never going to be a better district than your teachers").
- The district values its relationships highly and takes great care in recruitment and hiring the best people and building its capacity through induction, mentoring, coaching, and career-long learning.

• Collaboration is pervasive. "The work is horizontally and vertically connected, creating a seamless culture" (Fullan & Quinn, 2016, p. 44).

In the same vein, Hackney:

"Benchmarks on best performance—They are not content with 'good enough'; act quickly on detailed data and intelligence to provide school support; intervene speedily and rigorously to tackle poor or declining schools; promote innovation—development of teaching schools and information technology; develop expert capacity through partnerships working to help less-than-good schools" (Fullan, 2013, p. 105).

And Whittier:

"Has developed an effective structure to support collaboration within teacher teams and across schools, consisting of Course Leads, Department Chairs, and Curriculum and Assessment Coaches. . . . These groups have been instrumental in developing a coherent set of mindsets around the key priorities, practices, and strategies of the district" (Fullan & Quinn, 2016, pp. 5–6)

The presence of the Competencies *Focuses on team over self* (Competency 4), *Has a high sense of urgency for change and sustainable results* (Competency 5), and *Is committed to continuous improvement of self and the organization* (Competency 6) is evident. In short, the Framework and the Competencies are working together in a mutually reinforcing manner to ensure progress. The flow from focus to collaboration to learning in classrooms, schools, and across the districts puts the spotlight on high expectations tied to measurable impact on learning for all students. There is no "black box" because coherence and competencies force into the open (so to speak) pedagogy and its link to learning outcomes. Learning at last has been made explicit.

We said that there is an added complexity because learning is (and should be, in our view) radically transformed. We believe that literacy, numeracy, and high school graduation are no longer sufficient for today's world. The majority of students are bored by traditional schooling. Stress and anxiety are at an all-time high. The future of jobs, and even survival, is complex and in danger. Fullan and his colleagues have been working on new versions of learning that they call Deep Learning with corresponding new learning outcomes that they call Global Competencies (see Fullan, Quinn, & McEachen, 2018). These developments make the Framework and the Competencies all the more critical. Focusing direction would now include the 6 Cs/global competencies—character education, citizenship, communication, critical thinking and problem solving, collaboration, and creativity and imagination. Collaborative cultures and learning would now require the four pillars of learning—engaging pedagogies, partnerships, learning environments, and leveraging digital technology (Fullan, Quinn, & McEachen, 2018). But this only makes our model of coherence and the competencies all the more critical.

Securing accountability. In one real sense, the Framework and the Competencies, if employed up to this point, almost guarantee accountability. But let's make it explicit.

Almost 15 years ago, Richard Elmore (2004) said that no amount of external accountability will be successful in the absence of internal accountability. He added that internal accountability logically precedes external accountability. Internal accountability is defined as when the group doing the implementing holds itself responsible for progress and results in a transparent manner—transparent internally to themselves and externally to the system. (Note to the reader: We hope that the system that embraces the first three components of the Framework and the Competencies in a responsible, transparent manner will have already met the accountability requirement. What remains then is that the district will need to contend with the external assessment system.)

In the beginning of this chapter, we relayed the achievements of nine districts that were on a path of steady improvement. Still, things can go wrong. We report an example in *Coherence* (Fullan & Quinn, 2016) from Garden Grove, whereby the state tried to impose an ill-advised strategy and reporting requirement. The superintendent, Laura Schwalm, refused to follow the procedure and held her ground until the state backed off. Our view is that strong performance on coherence and leadership competencies increases one's professional and political capacity. You end up being able to hold your ground in both technical and power terms.

There is only one of the Competencies that has not yet come into play—*Builds external networks/partnerships* (Competency 7). We can see this all the way through, but it is especially critical when it comes to innovation (e.g., new ideas for deepening learning) and additional accountability. Trish Okoruwa at Hackney states:

"We engage national and international partners to identify excellence and innovation; to develop and promote local models of leadership that build on the success of practitioners; challenge and intervene; promote a culture of high ambition and no more excuses; and develop and promote excellent practice in the pedagogy of teaching, learning, and assessment" (Fullan, 2013, p. 104).

All of the districts were led by system leaders. They saw it as their responsibility, and to their benefit, to contribute to the bigger system and draw from it for their own good. As Lyle found in his leadership assessments, school principals who focused on instruction and stayed inside their schools were not as successful as those who focused on instruction and participated in outside networks. As we say, "Go outside to get better inside."

Leadership

We can be brief here because the essence of leadership for success was contained in the previous section—namely, leaders who are devoted to and skilled at coherence-making relative to the components of the Framework and are skilled in the Competencies. The skilled leaders develop highly effective teams and build the capacity of each team member through the Framework and the Competencies. In addition, there are three crucial cut-across qualities that these highly effective leaders evince:

- They constantly demonstrate tremendous *courage and resolve*. They don't back away from challenges. They don't give up. They inspire confidence in others.

- They *participate as learners* with staff in moving the district forward. They lead and learn and learn and lead.
- They are conscious from day one that one of their main tasks is to develop leadership in others.

One way to put it, as Fullan (2017) did, is that the leader's job is to develop collaborative leadership in others for six or more years to the point where they themselves become dispensable, leaving behind a legacy and capacity for the organization to carry on even more deeply than the present.

The leaders in this chapter, and others like them, face just as many potential distractions and disruptions as others. Yet they seem to manage them better. The question then is, how does one deal with leadership and management and stay focused on effective implementation of one's goals for achievement and come out on top? This is the focus of Chapter 4.

IMPLEMENTATION AND EXECUTION IS KEY

We have explained the power of coherence in building a successful district. You know the leadership competencies needed to be a coherent leader. Chapter 3, in addition to showing you how to apply the Competencies in relation to the Framework, provided the "how-to" to connect the Competencies with coherence-making when beginning to navigate the improvement process for obtaining sustainable results in student achievement. You should realize that how you apply the Competencies is both complicated and unique to the challenges and opportunities in each community.

Chapter 3 provided several examples of coherent leadership that have produced success for students and a vision for what coherence-making looks like, and how leaders were able to apply the Competencies to their journey.

Coherence and the Current Education System

When coherence is working and the leaders are effective, there is often a silent element at work. When leaders effectively implement and execute, we often fail to notice the talent and systems that provide the foundation for coherence-making. We have never seen a great leader who was not also an effective manager. Unfortunately, the lack of management skills that translates to the ability to implement goals in a timely manner to get results for student achievement is becoming a quiet but serious problem.

Our current education system was built to produce workers for the factories created by the Industrial Revolution. The workforce demanded that graduates be able to work on assembly lines and do what they were told. Everyone had a separate role and if they did their job, the corporation was successful. In fact, the current education system was redesigned to produce average workers and to discourage genius (Rose, 2017). The focus was on standardization and compliance. Administrators were trained to adopt a top-down, hierarchical management structure of "Taylorism" to manage the schools in a command/control model. A clear example of how schools needed to mirror the workplace was the introduction of bells between classes. The bells were established to emulate factory bells so as to mentally prepare students for their careers. The education system prepared students to follow orders and to be compliant. Those were the 20th century skills for the world of work in the 1900s. The management of schools was very important for administrators in education and keeping order/control was their primary function.

Management

Management was critical and leadership was not needed in a world of order and control. Management was defined as focusing on procedures and systems that control behavior and was not tied to vision and mission, which are leadership concepts. Ironically, as Mintzberg (2008) so devastatingly argues in *Managers Not MBAs*, the art of management has been lost as universities have striven for abstract theorizing and lofty images of leadership theory. MBA programs, Mintzberg concludes, are heavy on analysis, technique, and abstract strategy. The question for management is not about how smart you are in general, but rather about how grounded and insightful you are in practice.

Similarly, in *Hard Facts, Dangerous Half-Truths, and Total Nonsense*, Pfeffer and Sutton (2006) note that Google generates twice as many entries for "strategy" as it does for "implementation" as they conclude:

"Judging by mentions on book titles and search engines, figuring out what to do seems to be far more important than *the ability to actually do something—* such as operate the business effectively" (p. 135, italics in original).

Thus, leadership includes management—the capacity to implement. "Leadership is not about making clever decisions [in the abstract]. It is about energizing other people to make good decisions and . . . do things" (Mintzberg, 2008, p. 143). At the end of the day, it is about implementing good ideas.

Today's world of work is more focused on innovation, critical thinking, analytical skills, teamwork, creative problem solving, partnerships, and technology. The demands for school districts are to produce a workforce that is able to take their place in this innovative global society. Schools must produce students who are able to both think and do.

Leadership

Education has responded with a focus on leadership and specifically on instructional leadership. Many educational leaders believe that management was needed in the past and has no place in today's world of education. One superintendent told one of us that management isn't sexy. We must stop and realize—as Mintzberg so vividly warned us a decade and a half ago—that leadership in education today is becoming too abstract for many leaders and carries the assumption that the ability to implement effectively and bring in all stakeholders in support of desired results is obvious and not worthy of attention. This is a mistake if we want to meet our goals for students and be rigorous in coherence-making.

We want to recast management in education as the ability to execute and implement the goals for a district or school. The skills to effectively implement a plan need to be explicitly named and taught to leaders. It is a false dichotomy to place an "either/or" on management and leadership. We agree that management of the past is not enough for today's dynamic world. However, management does need to be directly connected to leadership in order to deliver on the vision of your school and the goals and strategies necessary to improve student success.

This chapter includes a caution: While our readers may seem ready and able to move ahead with coherence-making, there is one missing piece to the story. The skill base and the focus on effective execution are the foundation for sustainable coherence-making. Unfortunately, the national focus on instructional leadership has all but eliminated management from certification programs for administrators and training programs for leadership.

We are not saying that management is a separate discipline. However, we are saying that the skills and ability to implement a plan is an extension of leadership or a key function of how great leaders work. The ability to implement a plan with consistency and to build confidence in your staff so they can count on the follow-up necessary to reach your goals is another aspect of trust building that has been neglected.

Is There Really a Need to Bring Back Management and Increase Focus on Implementation?

Districts and schools have become reactive institutions when they need to be proactive in the thoughtful education and preparation of students for the 21st century. Being thoughtful requires time and perspective to think and to learn without constantly being interrupted. Unlike most businesses that have to meet the needs of a small list of stakeholders, school districts have a long list of people demanding their attention on a regular basis and the list continues to grow. We know schools must meet the needs of our students. These needs should be addressed coherently, not segmented in relation to each constituent's demand.

While trying to create a coherent district, the day-to-day barriers and distractions can be overwhelming. Most leaders want to build an excellent school or district that is steadfast in the focus on improving student achievement. However, the change and disequilibrium that are created in schools by trying to become coherent are immense and can be daunting to even the best leaders. In addition, the daily life in schools can break the concentration and the attention of professionals as they try to stay the course regarding the components of the Framework—focusing direction, cultivating collaborative cultures, deepening learning, securing accountability—and the application of the Competencies needed to create sustainable change—challenges the status quo, builds trust through clear communications and expectations, creates a commonly owned plan for success, focuses on team over self, has a high sense of urgency for change and sustainable results, is committed to continuous improvement of self and the organization, builds external networks/partnerships.

It never stops! Spend a day in many schools looking for any signs of clear goals and actions aligned with district plans, strong focused leadership, and clear measurements of student progress, and you will quickly become distracted. Without warning, a call for the principal to attend a meeting with the superintendent, a student behavioral problem, two teachers in conflict, an upset parent arriving in the office, or a technology breakdown occurs, and key administrators are pulled away from their focus on deeper learning. It is like a switch going off that results in a group of people who seemed focused and attentive suddenly leaving the room and starting to chase after the problem of the day. It seems difficult and almost impossible for a principal to stay proactive and not lose a day to myriad emerging problems. Day-to-day issues, problems, and the crisis du jour continue to frustrate educators' ability to focus on their core work—improving student learning. As one principal says, "I measure my day by determining if we made it through without any damage to our school or our students." He adds, "Sometimes I sit at home in the evening and try to figure out what I accomplished that day."

In our deep learning work, we are beginning to conclude that preparing students for college is no longer sufficient. Put another way, being literate, numerate, and a high school (or even college) graduate is not enough to become an effective member of the complex global world we are now living in (Fullan, Quinn, & McEachen, 2018). Effective leadership now requires engaging with increasingly wider elements of the environment—the first of which includes students, staff, parents, and the entire school community as partners. Therefore, our focus on management extends beyond the school building to parents and the community.

Parents, community members, school boards, local, state, and federal government, grant makers, and many others want the district to immediately respond to their concerns and needs. Add to the list the ever-increasing number of unfunded state mandates, policy changes with new legislators, new initiatives, and the increased challenge for educators to handle personal needs of students for safety, nutrition, and mental health services, it's no wonder our educational system is falling short of coherency.

The frenetic and reactive pace of education today has created a workforce that is unable to commit or stay focused on the strategic changes pivotal to improved student performance. Matt Manning, an elementary principal in Napa, California, provides an insight into the daily stress in education when he states,

"I must increase my ability to manage the discomfort of change for both myself and my teachers as a precondition for improvement. If not, all my focus on leadership, change, innovation, and improvement will increase the stress of my staff and undermine sustainable progress. If I delay, my desire to lead change would create even greater stress for me. Therefore, increasing our collective capacity to manage stress and handle distractions effectively will provide the essential conditions for sustainable improvement."

All change, including the most successful examples, include a degree of stress. Effective leaders acknowledge stress, but strategically develop a capacity for more effectively managing their schools, and thus continue to make progress despite barriers and distractors.

This chapter will now focus on how leaders can start building management practices and systems to form a foundation for creating coherence. Rather than being reactive, this proactive approach will promote the capacity of the entire school community to cease enabling practices and distribute accountability, responsibility, and greater concern for cherishing sustainable results for students.

Implementation and Execution Skills Need to Be Learned and Defined

Hope is not a strategy. Problems don't usually work themselves out over time. The change process evokes fear of the unknown, disruption to our day-to-day work, and an uncomfortable feeling that the skills for the current work may not be successful in the future. The fear of failure, the stress, and uncomfortable feelings attached to change is not a motivator. In fact, it is likely to deepen problems and conflict that move attention back to reactive behaviors and feelings of failure.

There are leaders who can push through the problems and keep moving forward. However, most leaders have been neither trained nor coached on exactly how to effectively execute their goals to ensure positive change.

So, what are these neglected implementation and execution skills that leaders need to learn and refine? They are

- Clarifying roles and responsibilities for administration, faculty, support staff, students, and parents
- Creating systems, practices, and accountability critical to smooth daily functioning, which includes bussing, attendance, scheduling, physical environment, student behavior management, substitutes, and the like
- Distributing responsibility and accountability for efficient and effective systems
- The ability to organize, anticipate, and plan both over the short and long term
- Communicating consistently and in a timely manner in ways that are understood by the entire school community
- Prioritizing and allocating time and resources to effectively implement goals
- Problem solving, conflict resolution, and crisis management
- Building change management strategies into school and district plans

Teacher Stress

How do these skills connect to emerging issues of stress in schools? Teachers' stress is growing nationally at an extraordinary rate. A recent study by the University of Missouri cited that 93 percent of teachers are stressed, and showed the negative effect of teacher stress on student performance. Kirtman's data includes the finding that teachers' ability to manage stress is very low. Even the data on high-performing teachers shows high levels of stress.

There are several aspects that are causing stress for teachers. Kirtman's work with teachers nationally cites lack of support on paperwork, forms, and compliance tasks as a major cause. In addition, teachers' lack of freedom and empowerment is also a contributor. The focus on improving management functions in schools and building real teacher leadership programs will help with the stress problem among teachers. This problem is both a leadership and management problem. Administrators building the capacity of teachers to lead and the power of teachers as resources for implementation will increase results for students and decrease stress.

This struggle between leadership and management happens every day in most schools.

The Importance of Focusing on Implementation: A Case in Point

A strong teacher leader in math wants her teachers to improve the results for students by visiting each other's classrooms to learn best practices. It seems obvious to her that her teachers will feel positive about learning from each other and her team will be excited to adopt new practices to help their students succeed.

Several of the teachers are immediately upset and feel their team leader is making them uncomfortable in front of their peers. They believe she thinks they are not good teachers. They get angry and say that she is a young teacher and has no right to criticize them since they have been successful teachers for 20 years. The teacher leader was trying to create coherence by setting clear direction for excellence, forming a collaborative culture, providing accountability for best practices, and creating deeper learning opportunities. She was acting as a strong leader by challenging the status quo and creating a sense of urgency. She was trying to manage her team by sharing best practices and fostering accountability for improving teacher practice for student learning.

The math teacher leader was very frustrated by the reaction of her team and did not understand why the teachers were resistant. She had not anticipated the effect of change on her team. She was adapting push competencies to move her team to excellence.

Why wasn't this working? The math teacher leader needed to focus more on implementation. While her goals were admirable, the process of implementation was underestimated. This is where leadership and management connect. The ability to motivate staff is a leadership quality and the process to ensure effective implementation needed more attention. The teachers were presented with a solution to a problem they did not understand and had no voice in the solution. If the teacher leader anticipated the reaction of her team and understood her own leadership style and the culture for change in her school, she would have created a different plan. The way to stop or at least curtail the reactive cultures in schools is to take the time to understand the change process and build in strategies up front to implement effectively. We learn through implementation and often need to adjust our plans based on reality. If one respects management as part of leadership, we can anticipate problems and make adjustments before we begin. Effective management will also save time!

The ability to anticipate change and build in strategies for effective implementation of that change into the school or department improvement plan will allow this teacher leader to curtail the reactive culture and maintain the focus on coherence.

Making Time to Anticipate and Manage Change: Reflective Leaders

All leaders need to anticipate and manage change and ensure that their plans incorporate strategies to prevent problems. Too often leaders say they have no time to think about the work, they just have to try to keep up. The best leaders do not get distracted and are able to build time into their schedule to be reflective leaders.

Recently, Lyle attended a meeting of principals in California to discuss their leadership development program. Some principals said they do not have the time to work on leadership until the district is able to take things off their plate. Other principals cited a lack of planning and reactive culture in the central office that did not allow them the time to work on leadership.

A follow-up meeting was held in the same district with the highest-performing leaders who were present but pretty quiet in the first meeting with their colleagues. One of the principals who is extremely successful stated that he was very frustrated during the meeting with his colleagues. He said that being an excellent principal started and ended with being a reflective leader. He said he faced the same challenges as his colleagues but did not see those as a barrier to success or a reason to not own his leadership development. He said he usually looks at himself and how he can understand his strengths and weaknesses and engage his leadership team in reflective work. Within the reflective time, he and his team confronted the concerns that his colleagues identified. His team developed strategies to anticipate problems and manage change and did not spend time complaining, reacting, and presenting excuses for not meeting their goals for students.

Reflective leaders are the most successful, but must look inwardly at themselves, their team, and their ability to manage and execute as key aspects of leadership.

Distractions to Coherence-Making: The Reactive Culture

The symptoms of reactive cultures that become distracted from coherence-making are numerous and include personality conflicts between teachers and staff, student incidents, last-minute requests for information, communication problems, sudden meetings that principals need to attend at the central office, separate uncoordinated requests from the central office to the schools, behavior problems with students, teacher absences, and so on. Every educator could add at least 5 or 10 more items to the list.

The long list of distractions also occur at the central office and includes sudden budget cuts from the state, new nonfunded mandates from the Department of Education, specific requests for reports from several school board members, community issues, problems played out in the media, and so on.

Another example of lack of management occurred when one of us was meeting with a leadership team and the principal on leadership development. The meeting time was never communicated to the team, which created schedule conflicts. Each assistant principal (AP) had a walkie-talkie so as to be able to respond to any crisis that might occur, and the principal attended the meeting for only five minutes because he had to leave suddenly because of a crisis. The crisis was that a student got sick in a classroom and the principal was paralyzed without his team to attend to the problem. The team realized that their reactive, high-stress environment was a problem. However, they said that it was a good day and that it is usually worse. This was a suburban district that was performing relatively well. A key management aspect of organization and communication was missing, which prevented the coherent leadership work needed for this school to be successful.

Things like this happen in schools all the time. The problem occurs at the school level and everyone reacts and the education process is disrupted. If you add in the directives from the district office, the environment becomes overly reactive. This creates tension at both a district and school level and often breaks down the relationship between the schools and the district office. The district office may often feel the principals are only focused on their schools, not being a system player. The principals feel the district office constantly derails their work and does not add value or help them with school-based challenges.

The reactive culture can pit superintendents against the state and federal government, school boards against the superintendent, the superintendent against the central office and, in many cases, the principals and teachers against the parents and students against teachers. This domino effect exists in most districts and many such situations receive more attention than making coherence successful.

Taking Steps to Build a Strong Implementation Foundation

As one learns and refines their skills to lead and implement, they must address the following steps to form a strong foundation for coherence-making. Following these steps will move your districts and schools to a life of proactive change and improvement and a way out of the world of reactive, frenetic days, which are too often accepted in schools today:

1. Build a strong office team—managing day-to-day
2. Central office leadership team as a service center to schools
3. Real teacher leadership
4. Parents as partners
5. Union leadership collaboration
6. Professional cultures—self-managing teams
7. School boards as part of leadership development
8. Two-way community resources/partnerships

Build a strong office team—managing day-to-day. A superintendent and principal need to develop a strong, empowered, highly effective and efficient team as a means to promote coherency, ownership, distributive leadership, and shared responsibility. The office support team, which includes the AP and the office staff (including office assistants and secretaries/administrative assistants), is essential to making implementation systems function efficiently and effectively preventing the unnecessary distraction of the educational leader.

Too often, there is a great deal of enabling behavior around doing for others what they can and should do for themselves. John Pierce, senior educational consultant and former high school principal, illustrates this practice in a story about his AP.

> While involved in an important meeting, the principal was interrupted by his AP, who unexpectedly burst through the door with a piece of paper and rapidly began to describe a problem he was having with a parent. He then handed the paper and problem to the principal and headed for the door. The principal stopped him, dropped the paper on the floor and said, "You have just left me your problem, kindly pick it up, summon all of your professional skills, and deal with it. If you exhaust your resources and cannot address it, by all means come back to me for help." The matter was resolved and an expectation regarding responsibility forged.

A principal's ability to manage his time and office staff should be a priority. The office team must fulfill critical responsibilities and cannot permit the day-to-day distractions to be passed along to block the work of focused leadership and management by the AP or the principal.

The AP's role in partnering with the principal is critical and must be thoughtfully discussed. Too often, this critical relationship is neglected and not maintained as a priority. When we see strong, effective leaders, we often see an empowered AP as a key force behind the success of those leaders. The AP should be just that—a force behind successful leaders—and not be relegated to simply handling student behavior as overall management matters. The AP can lead the implementation of certain goals, not just focus on tasks.

Pierce also emphasizes that the AP should work with teachers in clearly defining roles, responsibilities, and protocols regarding student behavior management. A mutual understanding between the AP and teachers regarding the difference between serious behaviors (behaviors that require that teachers immediately call for help) and less serious behaviors (behaviors that should be handled by teachers with a repertoire of strategies) proves very beneficial. This structure of expectations permits APs to be readily responsive to teachers with serious student behavior issues and not tied up with matters that are the responsibility of teachers. When teachers seek assistance with less serious behavior issues from the AP, they can clearly identify and benefit from the intervention employed by the AP. This also permits time for APs to take on other leadership responsibilities in support of the principal.

The principal and AP need to extend their leadership to build the capacity of their office assistant. The office assistant is a key partner for the principal in managing the day-to-day work in a school. This position is often neglected from a professional development standpoint. If we focused on management and implementation, we would respect the role of the office assistant more in education. In fact, many districts still use the word "secretary," which is rarely used in other sectors. It is time to upgrade our focus on the office assistant—key to managing derailments and a critical contributor to the role of leadership for a principal.

At the same time each week (Monday morning is ideal), the principal should meet quietly with her office assistant to discuss emerging issues, problem solve, and plan. One principal who was having problems in following through stated that she schedules a meeting every Monday morning with her office assistant. However, she admitted that the last three meetings were cancelled because of problems. These meetings must occur and only be cancelled in the event of an emergency. Identifying systemic barriers to regular meetings should be the focus of attention to make such meetings possible.

The principal and office assistant should each week review the schedule for the following week. In fact, it is advisable to review schedules one month in advance. Although your initial reaction to a one-month advance review of schedules might be that it wouldn't be possible, such a review allows for identification of key steps to be taken in order to meet important deadlines for upcoming events and paperwork. If we plan in advance, the day-to-day distractions will not derail the work.

The main reason to meet regularly is to help the office assistant understand the work of the leader, mentor the assistant, and enlist support and mutual feedback. The partnership becomes stronger as the office staff understands the work and the importance of the role in accomplishing the goals of the school. Office assistants that just do what they are told are not helpful to the principal's success. A strong office assistant can be a resource for coherence by anticipating problems and effectively intervening with self-sufficiency.

Once you are engaged in regular meetings, you can ask your office staff for their suggestions on systems, structures, and approaches to organize the work to prevent distractions from derailing the focus on the success of all students. Methods of managing the schedule, preparing materials in advance of meetings, clarifying roles and responsibilities, and reducing and managing e-mails are all important work to be discussed.

Principals often fall into the trap of trying to keep up with the demands of their jobs by working every evening and on weekends. The principal's work can be done during the workday if the distribution of management responsibilities is strong, the leader is focused, and a highly effective office team has been built. Preventing distractions involves a mental shift in attitude. All educational leaders need to dispel the notion that since students are involved, their work must be reactive and stressful. In fact, responding rather than reacting represents a far more effective strategy.

Recently, a principal was applying for a position as an assistant superintendent and missed three phone interviews, citing that her day got out of control and she lost track of time when dealing with a student issue. She further told the interviewer that they understood that life in schools is always like this and the interviewer should reschedule. The principal was eliminated from the search.

It is important to connect the reactive nature of the leader to the distributive management, initiative, responsibility, and capacities within the office staff. The office assistant who can only take a message instead of skillfully preventing and solving a potential problem, does not return calls promptly, and does not seem to understand what is going on in the school is a glaring symptom of poor team development in a school.

If you want to prevent or eliminate a reactive environment, build your office staff into a high-performance team. The superintendent and the central office leaders need to build their office teams to be able to handle many day-to-day issues. Too often, one of us deals with superintendents who do all their own scheduling, set up meetings themselves, and deal directly with most day-to-day issues without using their team to handle operational issues.

This process begins by the leader engaging support from the office team with paperwork, compliance tasks, scheduling, and any other potential distractions (such as calls from parents). The team needs to propose how they believe they can help and what the principal should delegate. The team may need training on norms for how they work together, efficient and effective office systems, customer service, conflict management, and accountability. A strategic investment in your office staff will have a sustainable impact on the organization and your time to address leadership matters. In some schools or districts, the office assistant can solve problems, refer issues to the right person, and provide needed information quickly. In other schools or districts, the principal does her own scheduling, all aspects of reports are controlled by the leader, or the principal spends every night answering e-mails.

Compliance requirements often derail the work of consistent improvement in schools. A paperwork- and complaint-driven culture removes teachers and administrators from having a critical dialog about the conditions for teaching and learning that must occur. Too often, the evaluation of teachers becomes a compliance process, and the time taken to write long evaluations limits or eliminates the time for effectively coaching teachers and staff in ways that produce immediate and sustainable results in the classroom. Developing sound management systems that reduce paperwork and compliance permits time for administrators to lead with strong implementation, which is key to making organizational coherence a reality.

One principal, who did not understand how to manage staff and attempted to do everything himself, attended a workshop on management skills. He asked the trainer for the right approach for deciding which meeting to attend when you are triple booked. The simple answer from the trainer was to avoid being tripled booked. The principal reexamined why he was consistently overbooked and now his office assistant is empowered to determine the scheduling.

With a strong office team to manage time and engage the right people in the day-to-day work to solve problems, the principal is able to build the capacity of the office team. Becoming a high-performance team is critical to distributing management, responsibility, and accountability and permits principals to focus on greater measures of student achievement.

Central office leadership team as a service center to schools. For coherence, the new requirement is that district leadership must function as a *team!* This means reducing silos at the central level, people having lateral knowledge of each other's work, and continually honing messages of consistency. This is done in interaction with schools in order to develop a common understanding of priorities and actions. Do school leaders have a "we-we" sense of effort with the district or a "we-they" relationship? Do school principals say that they get different messages from different departments at the district level? When school-level people talk about the goals, strategies, and progress being made by the district, is the message across schools consistent with what central office leaders say? This is the stuff of day-to-day management.

Educational leaders can no longer function independently in addressing the challenges of organizational change and development. Attracting, hiring, and retaining the very best people is part of the critical foundation for success. That is accomplished by creating a professional atmosphere where there is collaboration, teamwork, high expectations and generous support, shared decision making, and opportunities to contribute. Building a diverse leadership team with a clear sense of purpose allows leaders to tap into collective wisdom, exponentially extending their reach, and distributes leadership to a skilled group of people. It is important for the team to define their purpose and role in building the capacity of others throughout the school or district to advance student achievement.

The leadership team for a superintendent could be central office leaders or a combination of central office leaders and principals. The size of the school or district and number of administrators determines the formation of the leadership team. In a school, the leadership team should include APs, other key administrators, and teacher leaders (e.g., department heads or formal or informal teacher leaders).

The leadership team should provide direct, honest, and open feedback as an ongoing resource for the leader for sustainable school improvement. The team will need to engage in the same reflection as the leader regarding personal strengths and areas for improvement. The leadership team can also select a leadership competency of common focus for team development. The leader and the team should monitor and continually review their competencies and leadership development plan. Coaching for individuals and the team represent an invaluable resource for professional development and continuous feedback. As leaders and teams reflect and assess, it is important to apply the principles of adult learning to the process. Some areas to consider are training programs that are self-directed, practical, results-oriented, built on life experiences, motivational with high expectations, and always focused on why we all need to change (Knowles, 1988).

Here are two examples of superintendents who have developed leadership teams and achieved recognition in their field as "AASA National Superintendents of the Year."

In 2015, Terry Grier was a superintendent in Houston, Texas, and had recently retired. His enormous success in Houston is well documented and justly earned him this award and recognition. Terry believed his success was based on building a strong leadership team that could share the leadership and management of the district.

Mark Edwards, North Carolina Superintendent of the Year in 2013, is sometimes called the Innovation Superintendent since he is credited with starting the 1-1 initiative in technology. Mark had a clear (and we would say, reflective) explanation for his success. He stated that several years prior his focus would have been primarily on driving change and innovation from the top of the district. However, he was not seeing the genuine commitment of staff to the goals and outcomes that he wanted. He decided to change his leadership style to focus on developing the capacity of his leaders and forming a more highly performing leadership team based on a clearly articulated moral imperative. His role became more of that of a coach rather than as the driver of results. The result was that the district ranked among the top five in North Carolina for five years in a row. Student performance scores were high, despite the fact that the district was in the bottom five of the lowest funded in the state. He distributed leadership and developed the capacity of his team to effectively initiate and manage change. By increasing a strong sense of team ownership, initiative, and innovation instead of relying on his creativity and drive for success, the improvements were sustainable. The key shift for Mark was moving from being the sole driver of the change effort to building the capacity of the group within and across schools.

Fullan and Edwards have documented the shift in leadership style outlined by Edwards in *The Power of Unstoppable Momentum: Key Drivers to Revolutionize Your District* (2017). The crucial insight is that leaders participate as learners with others toward a common purpose.

To effectively drive change and improvement, district leadership must commit to school-based leadership and shift the role of the central or district office to becoming a service support center to the schools. This service center mindset does not mean that principals and teachers will make all decisions. Rather, it means that the central office models behaviors that show that schools are customers and that schools view students as customers. The measurement of success for the central office should always be the improvement of student performance in the schools. The notion of mutual vulnerability and interdependence in and of itself produces a more coherent organization capable of removing internal competition via collaboration and a greater capacity to empower students.

Central office and school administrators need training in the concept of customer service as it applies to schools. Too often, the central office rolls out incoherent initiatives from separate silos, not realizing the impact of distractions in derailing the primary work of the schools. Too often these initiatives have not even included input from the very people who must implement them. Each time an administrator needs some data or a report to send to the Department of Education, she e-mails the principal for the information. The expectation is that the principal drop what she is doing to respond immediately. If this happens frequently, the principal has less and less opportunity to participate as a learner in shaping the culture of learning in the school.

The capacity to be a service center to the schools begins with cultivating talent in the district. Central office leaders need to view their work as developing talent in the schools and integrating their focus area with the perspectives of principals and teachers. Too often, central office staff believe they must drive the work of their area and get directly involved in monitoring their agenda. If the focus of the central office is building capacity, they should be working collaboratively with principals on building teacher leadership. Simply stated, students cannot be empowered by un-empowered teachers, and principals cannot empower teachers without being empowered themselves.

Teacher leaders can have both formal and informal roles in school improvement work at the district and school levels. In one district, an aspiring leaders program for teachers drew 15 volunteers. The teachers were given a leadership assessment and actually scored higher than most administrators in leadership capacities. They genuinely wanted to help the district succeed and were not seeking more money or formal leadership titles.

The central office leadership team can enhance services to the schools by ensuring that highly competent administrators and teachers are hired. Hiring the right people and supporting them to work collaboratively are core aspects of leadership and capacity-building (i.e., building the skills of staff to increase student learning). If we want behaviors to change, we must have a strong hiring process that is valid and credible for all professional positions. The comprehensive hiring based on a set of coherent competencies such as Kirtman's 7 Competencies for Highly Effective Leaders ensures consistency throughout the district.

Intentionally creating diversity is the final and too-often overlooked aspect of hiring, capacity-building, and leadership development. This includes district decisions and the work at all levels from the school board to the classroom. Leaders must be comfortable discussing both race and gender in terms of its implications for leadership development. Equity, racist behaviors, gender bias, perceived institutional racism, and continuous microaggressions are major occurrences that can undermine fair and coherent behaviors in a district. When a Caucasian leader tells an African American leader that race should not be a factor in their leadership, the seeds for conflict, misunderstanding, and distrust are sown. Unfortunately, these disconnects surrounding race and gender occur every day and are not often discussed. Especially for leaders of color, race is part of everything they do every day, and the statement to separate race from other behaviors distances the person of color from the direction set by the district or school. This disconnect around race can exacerbate the "us versus them" mentality in schools. While we know that race is a very complicated issue in America, race discussions can become a normal everyday part of the work of leaders and a key aspect of genuine conversations at all levels.

The leadership and management skills require (a) continuously fostering diversity on the one hand and, on the other hand, (b) establishing and engaging in interaction in order to forge and establish what is being learned in and for the organization.

Real teacher leadership. Twenty-first century leaders face the issue of not having enough time, staff, or resources to remain strategic and consistently work toward coherence. A single superintendent or principal does not have the bandwidth to properly address the problems that occur each day while meeting the challenges of preparing students for the 21st century.

An approach to increasing management and leadership resources is to tap into the fertile soil of empowering teachers, distributing to them leadership, responsibility, and accountability. Increasing teacher leadership promotes ownership, motivation, and sense of community. In doing so, the principal has a far greater capacity to systematically control distractions and allow more focus on their leadership competencies for building a coherent school within a larger system and community.

Promoting teacher leadership has been a long-discussed and readily ignored imperative. This represents an example of the "knowing-doing gap" (acting consistently on what we know), and the time has come to unleash the power of teachers. This provides a management and leadership strategy to increase the capacity of the school to manage the day-to-day internal derailments and to expand the focus on results for students to include the voice and presence of the teacher. The distribution of management, leadership, and responsibility of teachers will impact results for students. The management aspect is the broadening of teachers in their role to handle problems and manage tasks, which will free up principals, APs, and others to lead.

Mutually defining effective student behavior management with clear roles and responsibilities would prompt enormous gains for everyone. A true measure of collaborative cultures connects directly to the derailing function of student behavior management issues. As mentioned previously, the expectation of teachers could be to handle the less serious problems experienced daily in classrooms.

The mutual development of a protocol and repertoire for teachers in addressing less serious problems (e.g., students arriving late to class, students who have not done their homework, students who fail to pay attention in class) will help teachers to develop the capacity for more instruction. The number of referrals to the AP will sharply be reduced and the teachers needing support will be identified. Setting teachers up with mentors and pairing highly skilled teachers with less experienced teachers are effective strategies for minimizing the distractions from student behavior. The entire systemic adjustment will yield greater consistency and coherency and will give administrators more time to address other systemic issues.

Leaders must focus on the individual needs of students and students' families. They need to be willing to drive change and improvement from the teacher up, not from the district down. A results culture needs to be established to make this new model work. A results-oriented culture defines and communicates to all constituencies what the critical competencies for students look like as they graduate from high school and seek post-secondary training and college and prepare for the world of work. The outcomes for students allow the elementary and middle schools to define their role in preparing students for their ultimate outcomes. Results can be defined in relation to a strong focus on personalized learning with knowledge of each student being clear and measurable in areas such as academic (assessments) and global competencies such as the 6 Cs (Fullan, Quinn, & McEachen, 2018) outlined in Figure 4.1.

We know that the top-down rolling out of multiple, often competing and incoherent initiatives to schools can be problematic. In fact, even the word "initiatives" is losing its luster and meaning and has added to the stress teachers already feel. Kirtman suggests using the words "high-impact strategies" instead of initiatives. Initiatives connote something new and continually bombard schools every year. Teachers become frustrated with the lack of staying with any new initiative for more than a year, even if it is working. Under the constant churn, there are many teachers who have initiative fatigue and want to turn back to past practices—practices that may not have been effective when employed or may not be effective in a rapidly changing environment. A high-impact strategy assumes that a mutually defined problem demands a mutually agreed upon strategy to address it. If the definition of "desired results for improving student achievement" and "impact" is clear, strategies that show progress toward goals will push aside old ineffective practices and new fads that are not results-oriented.

FIGURE 4.1

The 6 Cs: Deeper Learning

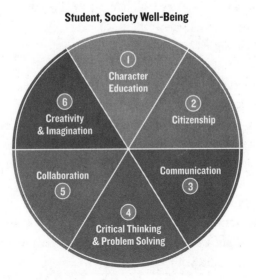

To implement personalized learning, differentiated instruction, formative assessments, flexible grouping, common planning, and other student-centered efforts, teachers need to assume leadership roles. Those who are experiencing success should be used to train those who are not. Teachers will need to be trained to be leaders and understand their role in increasing student achievement.

> An urban teacher participating in a leadership development session stated when she received a low score on a leadership assessment for achievement, "I never thought about my role in improving results for students in 20 years. I am not sure why I never thought of this as my role, but it never occurred to me."

This teacher would have thought about improving the learning of her own students, but apparently never focused on the collective responsibility of teachers to improve achievement for all students under their charge. Generally, teachers see their job as teaching the class and meeting the myriad needs and requirements that the district presents. Teachers often believe that the formal leader—the principal—is solely responsible for improving results for students.

We must change this dysfunctional paradigm. The power of all teachers being committed to improving student achievement will have far more impact than the superintendent, central office, and the principals. Teachers need to understand how to lead from their role as leaders of the school, not just from their role in the classroom. Learning how to influence with referential power is a skill and a behavior that has not been nurtured. Driving leadership and change from the classroom, teachers need to commit to their role as a key in achieving results. It is revealing to note that in a recent case study of the highly successful Whittier Unified High School District in California—a district with schools with large percentages of students living in poverty—Fullan, Quinn, and Adam (2016) traced the evolution of success and found that the key factor was the very high percentage of teachers who were in cross-district leadership teams. Central administrators were critical early on, but the teachers became critical for sustainable success.

A principal won an award for developing leadership within the faculty. However, when she looked deeper at teacher roles, confidence, and skills to lead, the contribution of teachers was not strong. As the principal carefully reviewed the results of a leadership survey that indicated that her teachers were not leaders, she was shocked. She asked her leadership team, "If I left today and a new principal came in and eliminated the programs we built over the last 10 years that have been successful, what would you do?" The teachers all responded that they would do whatever the new principal told them since that was their job—to follow the direction set by the principal.

To the principal's credit, this discouraging news motivated her to immediately work on developing teacher leadership with her entire team over the year. Now the teachers initiate projects to make changes in their classroom, review data and analyze and act on trends, and coach each other on both teaching and leadership skills.

Teachers, when empowered to lead, can solve many problems themselves or with the help of their colleagues. If the principal keeps solving problems for teachers, the principal will receive a new batch of problems every day. In this case, prior to the intervention of the principal, teachers had no incentive to solve the problems at their level.

The conversations among teachers that seem to lack focus and coherence are often not heard by principals and are rarely heard by superintendents. The people who hear all the conversations that teachers have about frustration, disagreement, lack of understanding and commitment to the district direction are . . . other teachers. Teacher leaders can be instrumental in beginning to turn around this unproductive culture to create coherent schools and districts. This begins with listening and understanding concerns and bringing issues to the table within leadership teams at the school level. Once these private conversations become more public, we can solve the problems that often create an environment that results in teachers not feeling safe to express their feelings and concerns. Speaking freely is now considered too risky for many teachers and thought of as getting other teachers in trouble. This must be a blame-free process that allows cultures to sort through change and learn how to gain equilibrium and maintain focus. Remember that effective leaders participate as learners, so that interaction helps identify issues that need addressing (Fullan, 2014). These school leaders also foster continuous teacher learning—teachers, individually and collectively, become collaborative professionals (Hargreaves & Fullan, 2012; Hargreaves & O'Connor, 2018).

The issue of trust often emerges quickly when discussing creating an environment where issues are discussed openly. You can't declare trust; you have to earn it (prove it) through interaction, and it must be reinforced through constant interaction. Trust, which often takes a long time to develop, can be lost over one incident or interaction. Schools and districts must address the building of trust through direct, honest, and open communication, interdependency, mutual respect, teamwork, transparency consensus-building, and the consistency of actions. Leaders must model the way for trust. As we build trust, we can better develop teacher leadership. Teachers who feel empowered to teach and lead with the support and coaching from principals will continuously improve and can then focus on establishing conditions for deeper learning with their students.

Parents as partners. Parents are the key partners we need in education to create sustainable learning beyond the school day into the home. Typically, the defensive and reactive environment in schools and districts is often influenced by the ineffective engagement of parents. In urban and rural environments, more work is done on developing the trust, participation, and critical support of parents in the educational process. In suburban settings, the parents tend to be either disconnected from or overly intrusive in their child's education. Either way, educational leaders must develop strategies and skills for managing the relationship with parents. Too often, the educator believes that he is in charge and does not see the partnership with the parent as important. This approach tends to push parents away, and the result is that the angry or frustrated parent pushes back. This push back is very distracting to the educator and can result in complaining to more senior leadership, resulting in a needless derailment.

A former principal in the northeast who would arrange to meet with parents before the parents met with individual teachers made a practice of addressing mutual vulnerability between school leadership faculty, students, and parents. The principal is vulnerable because she depends on faculty to provide an effective education to every child, teachers are vulnerable and need the principal to be an advocate for education and provide them with everything needed to teach and protect them from mindless criticism, and students and parents are vulnerable as they depend on the school to support the full development of every child. Acknowledging this mutual vulnerability makes it clear that, as a school community, we are interdependent and the best effort of any one without the other will fall short in the challenge of effectively preparing students for life in the 21st century. According to Bryk and Schneider (2004), the interdependent relationship builds trust to the extent that each member of this close community can reduce the sense of vulnerability and correspondingly increase trust with the other. Beyond trust, this deliberate attention to partnership promotes the authority of the school to carry on its work. In turn, this promotes understanding, confidence, and critical support from the school community.

We must realize that parents are critical partners in the process and should be treated much as if they were customers. The notion of customer is not popular in education circles. We should try to meet the needs of parents whenever possible and genuinely listen to questions, concerns, and even complaints. The skillful professional can approach this without overly engaging in the emotional issues. While in the end the parent may not be satisfied with your decision, your respectful approach, listening, and transparency regarding even-handedness represents a sound way to resolve conflict. Every organization should have a friendly protocol for those seeking resolution. Keep in mind that you want people to bring concerns to you rather than complain publicly with no resolution.

Parents will be true partners to educators if they understand the goals and outcomes for the school or district and how they can appropriately challenge the thinking of the educators. If they commit to the district's and school's goals, they are more likely to understand the need for consistency, coherency, equity, and structure.

Events such as parent–teacher conferences and parent nights are primarily focused on students. While the student is the core customer, we must remember the parent is also part of the customer relationship. Parent events should also focus on how the parent, teacher, and administrators will work together over the year. Reviewing the challenges and goals of the school or district informs and engages the role of everyone involved in success. If parents understand and support the school culture as partners, they will realize that how they interact with administrators and teachers impacts modeling and coherence. The next time the parent calls, there will be a clear approach to attend to the parent's needs that does not distract from the work of teaching and learning.

The breakdown of the parent relationships derails many districts and schools. There are many examples of angry parents that have assumed roles on school boards. In one case, in a more affluent district, the administrators and teachers all knew that if they did not like the direction set by the principal on a key issue, they could instigate the parent community to complain and usually change this direction.

It is also important to know your parents. Strong leaders tend to be transparent and vulnerable. This transparency can extend to knowing more about who their teachers and administrators are as people. It should also extend to knowing who the students are beyond the classroom. To further develop the partnership with parents, we should know who they are. Too often, principals are asked about the occupations of the parents or their interests and passions and have no knowledge. The positive talent of the parents to help with school or district issues is an often-untapped asset. The knowledge of who your parents are helps the leader connect personally, build trust, and enhance the partnership.

> A special education teacher recently invested more deliberate attention to partnership with the parents as customers. She was attending an IEP meeting with two upset parents, the principal, and the parents' attorney. The focus of the meeting agenda for the principal and the teacher was data and the needs of the student. The lawyer was ready for the battle with his data and demand to increase out-of-district services for the student.

The teacher's coach proposed a new approach: focus on the parents as customers. The parents were upset and expected the attention to be on the student. The teacher focused on the parents (resulting in the lawyer being out of his element and not a central factor in the meeting) and acknowledged their stress and the difficulty of raising their child and meeting her needs. The mother stopped the meeting when her husband became upset and asked to meet privately with the teacher. Once alone with the teacher, she began by admitting that she was frustrated and stated how much she appreciated the teacher's support. She said she would make sure that her husband supported the teacher and would trust that the child was in good hands. The child's needs were met and the district saved a considerable amount of money on out-of-district services.

Knowing the parents can serve you well in ways you may not realize.

A parent in a community was trying desperately to provide the best education for his daughter. He was constantly being told that his daughter was limited and that he should just focus on progress in her IEP. Although he was told about the regulations, he never had a conversation regarding how he could help his daughter to have a quality life despite her limitations. That parent was a CEO of a real estate company in the community. The district, in need of resources during severe budget cuts, reached out to him for help. While he was willing to help (because he believed education was very important), he was plagued by his daughter's situation. When the superintendent talked about focusing on achievement of all students whether or not they are in special education, the parent became animated and committed to the cause of education in the community. Someone cared about his child and children like her and did not read him a rule or regulation. Now he was pleased to help with the initiative to bring together other resources for the cause of public education.

One amazing example of connecting to parents and students occurs in a charter school network every day.

> At Public Prep Network (PPN), a charter school network in New York City that serves a diverse community, staff are trained to know who students and parents are; it is an integral part of the culture. PPN is committed to excellence for all students and realizes that knowing and connecting personally to students and their families is key to sustainable improvement. PPN has a protocol that all administrators and teachers follow every day: They greet each student personally. (Staff might welcome a student when they enter the building and they know about students' test results, attendance records (by saying, for example, to a student who was absent, "It is great to see you, Janelle. I know you were absent the last two days, but it is great you are here today," making the child feel both welcome and accountable, as the fact that they were absent was mentioned [which often results in improved attendance because the students see that the teacher cares]). Likewise, each parent is always warmly greeted when they call or enter the building. If the parent has a concern, it is in the record, and the administrator and a teacher might check in to see if the problem was addressed in a satisfactory manner.

Union leadership collaboration. Many principals and administrators complain that they cannot innovate and are thwarted by the teachers' unions in focusing on high expectations. Days are filled with grievances and complaints about unfair requests for teachers' time and efforts that are outside the contract. The districts and schools that have strong unions will tell you that "work to rule" (meaning that teachers will only do work stated in their contracts) and strikes are a looming fear in schools. Unions should be respected, but not feared. The contracts for teachers and administrators are written to ensure equity in treatment for professionals. Contracts are also a deterrent for unfair practices by poor administrators whose behavior feeds the need for protection. If you ask most leaders in education, contracts often go too far in undermining the reflective, innovative work and accountability that is needed by school professionals. We want teacher leaders but are concerned the concept can be thwarted by the teacher contract. In addition, teachers who are interested in trying new practices are fearful that the union will disapprove because innovation could put unfair pressure on other teachers.

One retired superintendent who was filling the role of a human resource administrator for a district stated, "The grievance process is the natural procedure for discussing change in a school and should not be viewed negatively. If a leader is acting professionally and promoting change, they should thoughtfully proceed and not be halted by fear that a grievance could be filed against their behavior." The grievance procedure is the formal process to discuss change. The removal of fear from change and grievances frees up a principal to move forward to develop a coherent school.

We have found unions will be reasonable regarding the change process if they are respected for their role and included early in the change process. In fact, the nine successful districts we featured in Chapter 3 all had productive relationships with their unions that got stronger over time. It is difficult to untangle cause and effect, but our view is that good leadership can be a route to positive and effective management-union relationships. California's Labor Management Initiative (https://cdefoundation.org/lmi/) represents a deliberate strategy for districts and unions to partner with the aim of increasing student achievement and has positive results to show for it.

In most states, unions are part of the fabric in education and the skills to work effectively with unions are critical to moving ahead on school or district goals. Union leaders should be included in leadership development work. Their role as leaders is very difficult and could benefit from training and support. Efforts to distribute leadership to teachers and to build truly collaborative cultures in schools that establish professional behaviors and expectations empower teachers and can minimize the negative aspects of unions holding back needed change and improvement.

Professional cultures—self-managing teams. We both hear about the lack of professionalism in schools and districts on a regular basis. Teachers are often criticized for worrying more about their contract and meeting the minimum requirements as a teacher than being dedicated to their students' success. In fact, the major reason for the evaluation focus in this country is a lack of faith in teacher professionalism. Lack of professionalism is also extended to support staff, support functions such as IT, human resources, finance, and maintenance, and other functions that are critical for the success of schools and districts. Our obsession with top-down leadership, monitoring progress, supervision, and accountability stems from our concern that the professionalism is lacking in education. Ironically, such micromanagement creates the very conditions that it seems to abhor. In *The Allure of Order: High Hopes, Dashed Expectations, and the Troubled Quest to Remake American Schooling*, Jal Mehta put it brilliantly when he concluded that "policymakers and legislators are trying to do at the back end with external pressure and accountability what they should have done at the front end (decades ago) with capacity building and collaboration" (Mehta, 2015, p. 7).

Building cultures of professionalism requires leaders to focus on their own development. Leaders who are reflective and vulnerable often create positive open and learning cultures. In addition, the structures of collaboration that involve decision making, meeting agendas and structures, hearing new ideas, budgeting, and teamwork must be aligned to collaborative cultures. Another aspect of culture-building is how people work with each other.

We see this culture-building as a three-legged stool comprising:

- Personal leadership behavior
- Group behavior
- Alignment of structures

How do we build a culture of professionalism in schools and districts? We say that culture is critical for schools to succeed. We think of culture-building as part of leadership. We believe that culture is important and key to collaboration in coherence-making. Moreover, we expand culture-building to include the practice of effective management and implementation. The development of professional behaviors is paramount to the development of a collaborative culture. The mutual development of a core set of professional and school community norms for the organization can serve as the basis for professional behavior. These rules of engagement and organizational or school community expectations clearly define personal and professional responsibilities, mutual respect, cooperation, effective communication, transparent decision making, and conflict resolution. Feedback, accountability, and consistent improvement are the substance of a truly collaborative culture.

John Pierce, senior educational consultant and former high school principal, states that teachers and principals are professionals and should own the definition, monitoring, and accountability for a professional learning community. This process begins with a common acceptance of what it actually means to be a professional and a community.

Pierce defines a professional as:

- Possessing knowledge, understanding, and skills that no one without education and training can bring to the position. This includes curriculum, instruction, and working effectively with a wide range of students, parents, and peers
- Accepting personal responsibility for consistent growth in the capacity to bring evidence-based best practices to all responsibilities
- Self-regulating behavior (i.e., never waiting to be told to do what professional responsibilities and standards require)
- Exerting respectful peer pressure on those who do not behave as professionals

John continues to say that all schools are organizations, but fewer are true communities. He uses a strategic process that gives a voice to every member of a school community in defining what is important in the way that people work together. That data is processed by a team of teachers into themes and then into professional norms, with complete vetting of all products. Each norm is then carefully reviewed and examples are drawn forth regarding what it actually looks like when a norm is being acted on and when a norm is not being acted on. While names are not used, the majority of faculty and staff uses this opportunity to bring to the surface unprofessional and unacceptable behaviors that derail collaboration, communication, trust, coherence, and credibility.

Ultimately, the professional and community norms are moved for adoption by strong consensus, codified, and used to provide feedback in transitioning to more professional and stronger community behaviors. The critical caveat is that after every voice has been heard and the norms formally adopted by strong consensus, there is neither a minority report nor undermining in any form by any member of the school community. In addition, the principal must be committed to being the lead follower of these professional community norms and be reciprocally accountable for modeling each of them.

The process also includes critical training in interpersonal relationships, listening skills, having direct conversations, and providing effective feedback. Too often, districts and schools try to develop norms without enough care and a genuine process. To be sustainable and to become part of the everyday work of a school, every voice must be heard and strong consensus must be achieved. A representative committee of faculty and members of the administration must take ownership of professionalism.

Schoolwide training and role-playing are used to practice and clarify self-regulation, peer feedback, and accountability. Ongoing audits must be conducted by the faculty and staff to assess continuous progress, inform as to areas in need of improvement or celebration, and to reinforce agreements.

And, in rare cases where it's necessary, formal sanction by the principal, coaching, and potential facilitation often resolve conflicts and should be tried before any sanction occurs. Accountability is not between individual personalities, philosophies, or positions but rather between shared school values/norms and unprofessional behaviors that are discrepant.

The function of this process is to distribute responsibility, management, leadership, and accountability throughout the entire organization. This lifts the burden of sole responsibility away from the principal or superintendent, who becomes the lead follower with more time to spend on strategic leadership work for the school and the district. In turn, teachers are empowered to be professional and are heavily invested in efforts to improve the school.

Adopting professional norms and reciprocal accountability (being accountable to each other for our norms, regardless of position) reduces organizational vulnerability and increases both credibility and critical trust between principals, faculty, staff, students, and parents. The principal models the norm that increases credibility with faculty. They model expectations for students and parents, increasing trust, confidence, understanding, and critical support for the school. When the behavior of all adults models what is demanded of students, students are far more likely to view high expectations for their behavior as fair, just, and not discrepant.

This in turn permits everyone to more effectively collaborate in meeting the challenges of constant change in an increasingly competitive world. Additionally, this process strategically addresses situations where the culture of the school is undermined by a small group of people who are committed to thwarting change and professional goals or strategies and fostering disruptions and divisions. Lastly, professional norms function as an effective, schoolwide source of civic education and the 21st century skills of teamwork and collaboration.

While some would argue that the ability to work effectively together will grow out of attacking the content of change, experience strongly suggests that without addressing the need to establish working relationships, the task of formidable change will not occur.

> One example, of many, is a high school in New England that was near the bottom of performance in its state for five consecutive years and seriously considering mass dismissal of faculty and administration. This norm process was the catalyst that re-engaged the entire faculty and administration. The empowered faculty focused on themselves in leading the way to critical change. The prevailing theme was that while no one was to blame, everyone was responsible for a more professional organization. The immediate results were dramatic, and within two years, the school achieved full accreditation status from the New England Association of Secondary Schools and Colleges and went on to receive recognition with a commissioner's award for student achievement and citation as one of the top schools in the state.

Behavior problems with students are distracting everywhere and can become a major concern. The strategies of short- and long-term approaches for dealing with behavioral issues are critical to preventing these derailments from occurring. The long-term leadership approach of restorative practices is systemic and moves beyond reactive approaches. Involving teachers in the process of preventing the need for discipline by increasing engagement of students in the classroom is also critical to managing behavior problems. Entire books are written on discipline and handling student and family issues to prevent and manage student behavior.

> A teacher in an urban district realized that she was not focused on student learning outcomes as she reviewed the results of a leadership assessment. The teacher admitted in a room of colleagues that every year she loses her focus on student outcomes when she sees the list of students in her classes. She immediately focuses on the behavior concerns and loses her energy to teach.

While this admission in front of peers is admirable, it is sad that this teacher was in her 20th year.

Based on this admission by a key teacher leader in this school and realizing that many other teachers felt the same way, the district increased the community's awareness of the importance of preventing and managing student behavioral issues. The school leadership team decided that they would focus together on a multiphased plan to stop turning over behavioral problems to the principal and AP. The two administrators spent almost every day chasing kids and never had time to lead. Sound familiar? The school leadership team wanted this reactive behavior to change. They asked their principal for support, coaching, and skill training. They also asked the principal to develop a strategy to work with parents and community organizations on this issue. The principal agreed that severe problems would still be an area of focus but would take up a lot less time and energy than they had.

If we want to look at the sociology of a district and how the adults interact with each other, we need to extend our work to the school board. The collaborative culture with professional norms needs to also be extended to the school board. Too many districts are losing superintendents, central office leaders, and principals due to an antagonistic relationship with the board. The current traditional board development process today is to define roles and hope that the board members stay in their lane and let the superintendent run the district. We promote that a true collaborative culture must be steeped in collaboration as the norm and that the board and superintendent learn how to collaborate first and define roles second. Board members are under pressure to become elected and often politics can result in saying one thing and doing another. This political reality and distraction to educational leaders must be recognized and attended to as a normal part of building a professionally collaborative culture. The traditional approach of defining the role of the board as separate first often creates more stress and distractions. Defining one's lane separately does not build skills of collaboration.

The creation of collaborative cultures that can act as a community over time to become coherent for the success of students and hold each other accountable for the behavior that they collectively have deemed necessary to model behaviors for students is essential for long-term success. However, the group dimension does not fully alleviate the need to focus on the individual. Each person is unique and must be a reflective leaders to fully contribute to forming coherent districts and schools.

School boards as part of leadership development. The principal, staff, and teachers frequently feel distracted by requests and initiatives that come down from the superintendent and central office. While the principal needs to develop skills in managing change and distractions in the school and the ability to manage up, there is still a problem with lack of focus on incorporating change strategies into plans coming from the top. In order to begin to curtail the top-down distractions that stop coherence, we need to begin our work from the top to change the mindset to help schools become coherent learning environments. The school board and the superintendent play key roles in reducing the distractions that trickle down.

We could talk about how schools can deal with these seemingly episodic intrusions, but we prefer to get at the source of the problem: board-superintendent relationships. Successful superintendents realize that this is not a control problem, but instead it is a leadership challenge. The school board needs to become a leadership team, partner with the superintendent, and focus on working with the municipal government and increasing community engagement in our schools. In *Local Governance in Education: Its Nature and*

Potential (in press), Campbell and Fullan have spelled out the mutual responsibilities of school boards and superintendents in developing a governance system based on coherence-making and moral imperatives and have provided guidelines and actions that would produce this mutual efficacy.

School administrators and teachers need to realize the pressure and stress for board members as they assume the role of being advocates for education in the community. To improve the board's advocacy, school administrators need to work collaboratively with the municipal side of the community. Administrators need to understand and support their board in gaining support from the community. The pressure on budgets and agendas from the community and municipality adds to school board members' stress, which can be passed down to the superintendent. The distractions that are caused by a lack of teamwork at the board level are legendary for both trustees and superintendents. Developing a coherent school district requires new relationships at the district level between trustees and superintendents. A collaborative culture needs to include structured time for boards and administrators, and even teachers, to work together. This collaborative model can only exist if there is a strong relationship between the board and superintendent, and the board functions as a leadership team. We realize that this is easier said than done, but a deliberate effort that is based on the premise that blaming either trustees or superintendents for bad relationships is a non-starter is required. Ideas and guidelines for developing more effective local governance are contained in *Local Governance in Education* (Campbell & Fullan, in press).

The takeaway for superintendents is to commit to the development of the board as a team. The superintendent needs to honor and value the relationship with each board member. The board is not a natural team, since they are often elected. Teamwork is critical at a district and school level. The same process of teamwork must be followed at the board level. Superintendents are often hesitant to commit to the teamwork process at the board level. They believe they can handle the work with the board. There are many superintendents who have made the mistake of believing that they can manage their board alone. Broadening the relationship between the board and the learning agenda of the district is always a good idea, but it must be done through joint work on the part of trustees and district leaders.

In the town of Wethersfield, Connecticut, the coherence work has included the school board. While there had been a history of tension between the board and the administration, the teamwork toward common direction is clear both within the board, across party lines, and with the administration. Since this work needs to be sustained over time, the board has quarterly retreats on achieving excellence for all students and continued teamwork, especially as members change through the election process.

In sum, the superintendent needs to build on the teamwork with the board and create a sense that we are all in this work of educating our students. Virtually all districts that have been successful, such as the nine outlined in Chapter 3, have figured out this key insight. Effective local governance remains one of the unfinished chapters in school improvement. It lies at the heart of effective implementation. For us, local governance remains a difficult but largely untapped source of school and district improvement.

Two-way community resources/partnerships. The final step is to build a strong sense of teamwork with the municipal government and the community. Too often, the relationship between the municipal and the educational system is adversarial or ignored altogether until a problem arises. The main cause of the tension is usually budgets. The municipal leaders often resent the high proportion of community resources that are allocated to schools. The municipal government can also resent their lack of control over school budgets. This tension is both a leadership and management issue. The leadership aspect is the superintendents seeing their role as community-wide and focusing on the health of the community. The management aspect is figuring out how finite resources can be allocated to meet district goals and create community success. Collaboration and attending to the sociology of a district is to connect to the community and the municipal government. Too many leadership programs focus only on instructional leadership and how the schools need to stay focused internally. We must remember that the community owns the district and the schools. School officials and municipal leaders need to learn how to understand each other and work together. The municipal government is always in competition with the schools for funding and attention. They cannot be demonized, since they are also committed to the community. We must learn how to collaborate with our community agencies and key community leaders.

Although we don't have the space to address the much-neglected topic of school board–superintendent relationships, in *Local Governance in Education: Its Nature and Potential*, Campbell and Fullan (in press) show how the Framework, systems leadership from trustees, and senior administrators working together can make a profound difference for the communities they serve, including staff and on student learning.

The creation of truly collaborative cultures that can act as a community to become coherent for the success of students and hold each other accountable for the behavior that they collectively have deemed necessary to model behaviors for students is essential for long-term success. One superintendent in Texas focused on the relationship of the schools to the municipality and community in a very creative and comprehensive manner.

> Karen Rue worked to bring together all internal and external groups with the formation of academies. She did not start in the traditional place with her administrators and principals. She started with support staff. Karen states, "We started with the HR Academy. It was comprised of 36 lead paraprofessionals from every campus and every department (maintenance was included) of the district, with a new 36 attending the next year. The Human Resources department took the lead in designing the academy. The initial 36 identified were invited by me to participate, and principals/departments were made aware of the importance of freeing time for their office staff members to attend. (As you know, principals feel lost without their secretary/office manager/receptionist on campus.)
>
> "The HR Academy grew out of a need to support campus and district front office staff as they interacted with community members, parents, staff, and other departments. I felt that it was important to be able to be a one-stop shop to the greatest extent possible. For

example, if a teacher asked the office manager about a budget item, or wondered how to request a long-term health leave, we wanted the office staff to be able to offer first-glance information and know who to direct them to to discuss details in depth. We wanted front office and department staff to feel confident that they could handle any situation.

"These folks take the brunt of a parent's initial frustration, a staff member's concern, or a community member's ire that the 2nd grade flag crew flew the Texas flag out of order, again! I remember telling them that they were the front line. They performed 'triage' for the campus or department and had it within their hands to quickly diffuse a situation. They were the ones to decide: this can't wait. This issue can get a quick answer with follow-up scheduled later. These issues mean find the principal now, keep the person talking, and pray they aren't texting media while I try to calm them down. In short, they were our first ambassadors to staff and community. They were important to our success.

"HR Academy members were provided training designed to enhance their capacity to support and encourage the promotion of a positive campus culture, support their decision making as they faced everyday encounters with parents and staff, and as a vehicle to recognize their efforts. They saw paraprofessionals as envoys of goodwill and information sharing.

"They took pride in helping solve problems/answer questions without sending someone on a scavenger hunt through district offices looking for answers. A culture of service, getting answers from the first person you ask, was the beginning. And they had fun with a board meeting recognition ceremony honoring their graduation from the academy. A celebration of their learning. Long story short, they loved it. They felt empowered; they felt that they succeeded each time they could take care of a need without sending the parent or staff member on a scavenger hunt through district offices looking for information."

Karen did not stop with the support staff. She continued the process of collaboration and teamwork to reduce stress and reactive behavior and distractions. Karen continued,

"Next, we wanted to encourage teachers and parents in their support of public education, and Northwest ISD in particular. We reached out to an organization known as Friends of Texas Public Schools to lead in the creation of two new academies: one for professional staff and one for parents. The goal was to grow their teachers' and professional employees' understanding of their important role as ambassadors for Northwest ISD, and to create a cadre of vocal parent advocates for NISD."

These two academies were opened with a rather unapologetic message from Karen: the intention was to see them become active advocates for public education—in their schools, their homes, and their interactions with the public—wherever they might find an opportunity to share news about their school district. A significant part of the sessions centered on building their knowledge of school district operations and their understanding of legislative action. Throughout it all, the culture of NISD as a service-oriented organization permeated. Karen's teamwork and customer service process resulted in support from her community when funding was cut. People rallied around the district and raised money to support key programs. Northwest ISD was a very high-performing, coherent district for all students and the whole community.

•••••

Understanding coherence, leading coherently, and building a foundation with strong execution skills and behaviors will ensure that your journey to success will be able to withstand all the challenges that a day in education can present. This chapter is crucial to your path forward to understand how to reinvent management in education: going beyond typical command, control, and compliance to fully execute the vision and goals of your district in a seamless manner. This chapter also counteracts the tendency to ignore implementation details and leave it up to schools to figure it out. Either from by-products of micromanagement or the fallout of being laissez-faire, educators end up burning out and being overly stressed. Our alternative addresses implementation directly in partnership with the various partners. By engaging teachers as leaders, we will increase results for student success and help the principal build strong management bandwidth. In addition, if you incorporate the areas of building strong office and leadership teams, working closely with parents, connecting to your unions and boards as partners, and reaching out and using community resources, you will be able to manage the day-to-day distractions and stay the course to coherence.

Remember, "management" is not a dirty word. While leadership steals the show for most training and publication, the ability to implement, in partnership with diverse others, is the secret sauce that makes great leaders succeed!

LEADERSHIP FOR THE FUTURE

The nature of leadership is changing because the environment is changing. Climate change, technology, and the uncertainty of the future of work, rapidly growing inequity, increased anxiety for all age levels and SES groups all make for a more complex and, in many ways, dangerous world. Potentially, more opportunities exist, but these are also layered in more complexity. We can approach this growing complexity in three ways:

- Leadership for coherence-making
- Honing your leadership competencies
- Leadership for deep learning

Note
The first two are stabilizers and the third is built on continuous adaptability.

Leadership for Coherence-Making

In a companion workbook to *The Taking Action Guide: Building Coherence in Schools* (2016), we (Fullan, Quinn, and Adam) developed protocols—33 to be exact—linked to the Framework to enable applied use and development of the Competencies and the subskills. Protocol 18—Lead Learner Competencies Protocol (see

Figure 5.1)—comprises three main sets of leadership competencies: modeling learning, shaping culture, and maximizing learning.

> Let's assume that you have just been appointed to a new position as principal of a school with a mandate to turn around or otherwise significantly improve the quality of the school. Where do you start? Let's take James Bond (yes, that's his real name) of Park Manor Public School in Elmira, Ontario. Bond arrives as principal of a rural school west of Toronto comprising 300 students and nine classrooms with teachers having little to do with one another with respect to instruction. Although the atmosphere is positive, people like each other, and social interaction is very friendly, academic performance has flatlined.

What would you do in year one if you were Bond and were committed to increasing learning? Or we can head out to a school in the Garden Grove Unified School District in Anaheim, California (introduced in Chapter 3) and visit Michelle Pinchot:

> Michelle arrives at her first school principalship: K–3 Peters—a very large early learning school with more than 600 students. K–3 Peters has a high percentage of (mostly Latino and other minority) students in poverty who have been stuck at below-average literacy for as long as anyone can remember.

What would you do to change the situation for the better? Or we can follow Michelle five years later when she moves to Heritage Elementary, also in the Garden Grove Unified School District, whose size and issues are similar to those of K–3 Peters, and which is also "stuck in neutral." Where does Michelle start?

Fullan has worked with all three of these schools—all have been successful in shifting from being stagnant in morale in student learning to becoming highly successful in relatively short periods of time.

FIGURE 5.1

Lead Learner Competencies Protocol

Learning Leadership

Purpose
- Assess the attributes of Leader Learner Competencies and identify areas of growth.

Lead Learner Competencies Protocol
This protocol allows individuals to reflect on strengths by citing evidence and then identifying areas for growth.

Complete this chart individually and reflect on your strengths and areas for growth.

Competencies	Criteria	Evidence
Modeling learning	• Participate as a learner • Lead capacity-building • Make learning a priority • Foster leadership at all levels	
Shaping culture	• Build relational trust and relationships • Create structures and process for collaborative work • Support cycles of learning and application • Engage others in solving complex problems • Resource strategically	
Maximizing learning	• Focus on precision in learning and teaching • Establish a small number of goals • Create a clear strategy for achieving goals • Orchestrate the work of coaches, teacher leaders, and support personnel around student learning • Monitor impact on learning through collaborative inquiry	

Source: Fullan, Quinn, and Adam (2016).

Note

You can review the Park Manor Public School and K–3 Peters cases on video at www.michaelfullan.ca and can read an article about the Heritage Elementary case in *Educational Leadership* (Fullan & Pinchot, 2018).

Despite some differences in the nature of the schools, the essence of the change strategy was similar. Although the two leaders—Bond and Pinchot—basically signaled that the status quo was not acceptable, they did not come across as judgmental. They stated that they wanted to establish a climate of trust wherein it was okay to make mistakes and admit you don't know the answer to something, and that they would in the first year move slowly and focus on building relationships.

We can use the *Lead Learner Competencies Protocol (Protocol 18)* (see Figure 5.1) to explain Bond's and Pinchot's actions (noting that it is no accident that their actions and the protocol are congruent because we derived the protocols from successful practice, including those of Bond and Pinchot). Both leaders modeled learning, shaped new cultures, and focused on maximizing learning and results.

Modeling Learning

The short form of *modeling learning* is to think of establishing new behavior by naming it, modeling it, and monitoring it. It is not a private matter. Leaders must be transparent. Both James and Michelle said to staff at the beginning of year one: it is okay to admit you don't know how to do certain things; I will also do that when I am not sure. I will take out time in year one to build trust, examine data on student learning, build relationships, and so on (what Lyle and I call "start slow to go fast"). But my overall direction and commitment is to take specific action, begin to get results, and build on them.

In Park Manor and K–3 Peters, improved results began to be seen in year two and began to accelerate in years three and beyond. In the case of Heritage Elementary, Fullan and Pinchot conducted a small, real-time experiment: As soon as Michelle was appointed and before she arrived at Heritage, Pinchot and Fullan sought to see how long (really, how fast) it would take for the school to make substantial progress if Pinchot used what she knew and customized it to Heritage's situation—and they found that it took 18 months (see Fullan & Pinchot, 2018).

Both leaders modeled learning. They made it clear that change was needed, and that they would work with staff to make this happen. They moved slowly but steadily. They made leading and learning a priority, and above all, they participated as learners—two vital concepts of which are participate (be there) and learn (day in and day out). They made learning a priority in two senses of the work—that is, adults as learners and students as learning (literacy, for example). They developed leadership among the staff. (We have since noticed that one of the most powerful indicators of likely impact on student learning is the percentage of teachers in a school who are in leadership positions [i.e., leading and being on action committees].) In both cases, at least half of the teachers became leaders. This results in two powerful phenomena:

- There becomes a critical mass of staff who are engaged in leading and learning, thus having a coordinated impact.
- The critical mass soon represents a cadre of leaders, thereby increasing the capacity of the school to carry on after the incumbent principal leaves.

As we say, the main goal of a leader is to develop a focused collaborative culture for five to seven years or so—to the point where the leader becomes *dispensable* (although this may seem an odd way to put it, all leaders leave sooner or later, and the capacity they leave behind is just as or more important as what they accomplished while they were there). Lead learners are conscious that they are doing *both*—developing staff who are engaged in leading and learning and increasing the capacity of the school to carry on after their departure—and the beauty is that they are synergistic (i.e., doing one does the other at the same time). The rest of Protocol 18 further exemplifies what we are talking about, and both James and Michelle were role models in this respect.

Shaping Culture

James and Michelle were aware of and explicitly committed to the second lead learner component—*shaping culture*. Fundamentally, leaders must set as an explicit goal with staff that we are not just "changing this or that" but rather we are "changing the way we do things around here" and that this change represents a (small) combination of vital components that will produce a new coherent culture, as denoted in the five elements of shaping culture—building relational trust and relationships, creating structures and processes designed for collaborative work, supporting cycles of learning and application, engaging others in solving complex problems (joint problem solving), and acquiring and using resources strategically.

Maximizing Learning

Modeling learning and shaping culture was in the service of maximizing learning. Effective leaders build on the solid start by going more deeply into the changes that will make more of a difference. This typically occurs in year two and beyond. It is about *maximizing learning*, which requires an interrelated set of actions: establishing a small number of goals; focusing/zeroing in on precision of instruction (recall that precision is good and that prescription is usually bad); creating a clear strategy for achieving goals (ensuring that the strategy is clear, sound, and well understood); orchestrating/coordinating the work of coaches, teachers leaders, and support personnel (the support system) around the specific capacity-building needed (student learning); and monitoring impact on learning through collaborative inquiry (again, remember that the primary purpose of examining impact data is to provide feedback to your own group about how well you are doing and what needs attention and that understanding and improving progress is the goal at this stage).

In effect, the work of the lead learner that we described is the leader's perspective of how to go about coherence-making that is required for the overall Framework (see Figure 5.2).

Focusing direction consists of deciding on the small number of goals to be pursued. The modeling is in relation to those goals and getting people initially immersed into the content of the direction. Cultivating collaborative cultures builds on the direction through capacity-building. As one goes deeper into collaborative work, the specifics of instruction and learning become increasingly evident and become the focus. It is at this point that the press for deepening learning becomes a reality. Evidence of progress or not comes into focus

FIGURE 5.2

The Coherence Framework

and that, in turn, leads to greater emphasis on "how far are we getting." This is the beginning of securing accountability because it consists of internal accountability, which, with Elmore (2004), we see as a prerequisite to engaging in and addressing the demands of external accountability.

The net effect is that the Framework gets established as the guiding modus operandi of the school or district. This is the job of the lead learner especially in the first three years, after which coherence-making becomes the reinforcing capacity of the system.

Honing Your Leadership Competencies—the Competencies

There are two considerations to address. First, review and understand the Competencies and how you personally might fare with regard to each one.

Second, examine how the Competencies might play themselves out in terms of push and pull and related combinations and the Framework.

The Competencies are not meant to be addressed in a one-by-one linear fashion. They should be viewed as a set. Examine the Competencies and the 36 competency subskills (see Figure 5.3).

Yes, there is a lot there, but they are clustered into domains (a competency and its subskills constitute a domain), and once you learn how they feed on one another, they become more memorable. Still, you must appreciate each one.

Competency 1

Challenging the status quo is difficult for two reasons. First, by definition the status quo has been around for a while, and many people take the at least tacit stance that this is the way things are. It is very difficult to shake them out of this tendency. Second, our guess is that at the beginning you may not know *how* to proceed. In fact, we suggest that you not be too sure of yourself about strategy. Instead, you need to convey that strategy will be worked out jointly with members of the organization and that you have some ideas about how to approach the situation but will need other ideas. John Kotter made a distinction between "focused urgency" and "frenzied urgency" (multiple ad hoc initiatives that come and go at a rapid pace) (2008).

Competency 2 and Competency 3

Building trust through clear communications and expectations and *creating a commonly owned plan for success* are the sets of actions that cultivate and persist with focused urgency. Working through these developments is difficult for leaders in a hurry. The irony is that fast change with poor implementation generates much less change than slow change with good implementation. Shortly we will make the point that you don't have to trade quality for speed. With care in the first six to 12 months in relation to the first three competencies, you establish the conditions for accelerated change (our "go slow to go fast" advice). We have observed and been part of substantial change that occurred over a two-year period and was still going strong. So, are you good at getting people on board for collective commitment to getting effective change off the ground?

FIGURE 5.3

Kirtman's 7 Competencies for Highly Effective Leaders and the 36 Competency Subskills

1. Challenges the status quo (Push)
   —Challenges common practices and traditions if they are blocking improvements
   —Is willing to take risks
   —Delegates compliance tasks to other staff
   —Does not let rules and regulations block results and slow down progress
   —Focuses on innovation to get results

2. Builds trust through clear communications and expectations (Push)
   —Is direct and honest about performance expectations
   —Follows through with actions on all commitments
   —Makes sure there is a clear understanding based on written and verbal communications
   —Is comfortable dealing with conflict

3. Creates a commonly owned plan for success (Pull)
   —Ensures that people buy into the plan
   —Creates written plans with input of stakeholders
   —Develops clear measurement for each goal in the plan
   —Monitors implementation of the plan
   —Adjusts the plan based on new data and communicates changes clearly
   —Creates short- and long-term plans

4. Focuses on team over self (Pull)
   —Seeks critical feedback
   —Supports the professional development of all staff
   —Commits to the ongoing development of a high-performance leadership team
   —Creates a team environment
   —Empowers staff to make decisions and get results
   —Hires the best people for the team

(continues)

FIGURE 5.3   (*continued*)

Kirtman's 7 Competencies for Highly Effective Leaders and the 36 Competency Subskills

5. Has a high sense of urgency for change and sustainable results (Push)

    —Is able to move initiatives ahead quickly

    —Can be very decisive

    —Uses instructional data to support needed change

    —Builds systemic strategies to ensure sustainability of change

    —Sets a clear direction for the organization

    —Is able to deal with and manage change effectively

6. Is committed to continuous improvement of self and the organization (Pull)

    —Has a high sense of curiosity for new ways to get results

    —Is willing to change current practices for themselves and others

    —Listens to all team members to change practices to obtain results

    —Takes responsibility for their actions (no excuses)

    —Has strong self-management and self-reflection skills

7. Builds external networks/partnerships

    —Uses technology to expand and manage a network of resources and people

    —Understands their role as being a part of a variety of external networks for change and improvement

    —Sees their role as a leader in a broad-based manner outside the work environment and community walls

    —Has a strong ability to engage people inside and outside in two-way partnerships

Competency 4

All along—from day one—you will be figuring out how to focus on the team rather than on yourself, so to speak. This is about what Andy Hargreaves and Michael Fullan (2012) have called developing the "professional capital" —the human, social, and decisional capital—of teachers.

Human capital is about individuals and consists of hiring, cultivating, and (yes) making changes in leadership positions as you build the best team. Individual quality, while necessary for success, is not a sufficient factor for success (i.e., you can add quality individuals to the organization until the cows come home, but a bad culture will eat them up faster than you can produce them). This is why *social capital* (the quality of the group) is essential. Hargreaves and Fullan have found time and again that individual autonomy combined with "collaborative professionalism" is a winning combination (see Fullan & Hargreaves, 2016; Hargreaves & Fullan, 2012; Hargreaves & O'Connor, 2018). This domain—*Focuses on team over self* and the subskills—is where leaders, along with staff, "participate as learners" to build a culture of connected empowerment that is in the service of effectively challenging the status quo.

Competency 5 and Competency 6

The third dimension of professional capital—*decisional capital*—takes us directly to Competency 5—*Has a high sense of urgency for change and sustainable results*—and Competency 6—*Is committed to continuous improvement of self and the organization.* Successful systems are not just concerned with results. If anything, they are more focused on which practices are *producing* results. We talked earlier about "precision" of practice, which we consider to be more important than prescription. We find that if certain practices are precise, they will get results. While you may still need to accelerate results when there is a large achievement gap, you will not need to impose them. Most teachers will adopt "precision of practice" if it is effective in relation to student engagement and learning. If this process occurs within collaborative cultures, peers will influence one another to pursue practices that work.

Prescription, on the other hand, generates resistance or thoughtless compliance. Commitment to continuous improvement is not just, "Are we making progress?" (although it is that), but also, "Now that we are getting somewhere, what might be done to get even better?" This invites innovation, listening to diverse others (the mavericks, students, etc.), and new actions.

Competency 7

Building external networks/partnerships is tricky. Intuitively, one can think that staying focused internally—let's call it "stick to the knitting"—would leave you better off. One would be wrong. While it is true that if leaders spend most of their time networking outside that internal development will suffer, Kirtman found something more refined: principals who focused on instruction inside, and did not connect outside, had poorer results than those who focused inside and buttressed it with specific external connections. "Go outside to get better inside," we say. This domain also enables what we have called "systemness." The role description we have in mind is that school leaders have a responsibility to learn from the bigger system (district, state, etc.) *and* to contribute to its betterment. One way of stating this is that your school cannot get better for long if the context (again other schools, district, state) is not improving.

• • • • •

To conclude, for starters, we suggest that you do a run-through of the Competencies to get a sense of where you stand—that is, determine in what competencies are you strong, in which are you weak, how the competencies interrelate, for better or worse in your case. You will then have the outlines of an agenda.

Push and Pull

Great leaders read situations and people. They build strong relationships and seek feedback from all sources. These attributes give them insight into when to push or be assertive and when they need to draw people in. In Chapter 2, while some of the Competencies were categorized as "push" and others "pull," in fact, all can either push or pull. For example, challenging the status quo is clearly pushy, but sometimes it can operate more as a pull (such as when a group examines outcome data and is drawn to how poorly some students are doing). Let's return to principal Michelle Pinchot at K–3 Peters in Garden Grove Unified School District:

> Shortly after getting to know the teachers, Michelle looked at literacy
> data that enabled teachers to see that some students were not doing

as well as others, and Michelle and the teachers began to acknowledge that perhaps there was a way to move some of the students forward. (Throughout this book we have referred to "push" and "pull" competencies. While some of the competencies have a central tendency to do one or the other, most of the competencies can both push and pull [i.e., a push-pull strategy].) Michelle used a push-pull strategy when she created three committees of teachers—one each for management, data, and curriculum and instruction. She sat on all three committees and had teachers chair each group where teachers determined the specific purposes and actions of each group (we call this "use the group to change the group," not a manipulative ploy but an open attempt to get teachers' input and commitment, individually and collectively). Within four years, teachers saw that literacy scores climbed 11 percent in a single year—the first time the school had ever experienced double-digit increases in a single year.

In coherence terms (referencing the Framework): purposes and goals become focused and specific, collaboration gets more deliberate, teaching and learning in the classroom is a lot more precise, and outcomes are more evident and more positive. Internal accountability talked about and shared as outcomes becomes more positive. There is greater confidence in relating to external accountability.

Overall, we see how the Framework and the Competencies feed on each other as mutually reinforcing factors. You can't get very far with coherence-making and the components of the Framework without the Competencies and you can't focus on the system effectively if you are operating in the absence of an integrated framework.

Leadership for Deep Learning

As we project to the future—or we might just as well say the present because the future we are talking about is already upon us—just about every global force we can identify is in unpredictable flux:

* *Climate.* Whatever side you take, it looks like a crapshoot. No one should be confident that we are safe going into the future.

- *Jobs*. Fewer jobs, more robots, and utter pessimism about what might be available.
- *Economics*. For the past 40 years, inequity of income and school performance has occurred in almost every country and is certainly overall increasing rapidly.
- *Social cohesion*. We have more access to more people in more far-flung places in the world. We have more digital connections, but they are increasingly superficial. One thing that is not increasing is positive feelings toward each other. Trust and social cohesion are eroding on a large scale.

In other work that Fullan and his team are conducting, these emerging scenarios have led to new considerations with respect to what might be needed in public education for the immediate future, and consequently, for leadership. We have called the new developments *deep learning* (Fullan, Quinn, & McEachen, 2018). The gist of the development is that basic education concerning literacy, numeracy, and high school graduation—and even college graduation—may not be sufficient for coping with the world that is now emerging. Additionally, what we call "global competencies" (what we refer to as the 6 Cs—character education, citizenship, communication, critical thinking and problem solving, collaboration, and creativity and imagination) will be required.

We also see and are developing radical changes in pedagogy that we call "deep learning." These changes in pedagogy include partnerships (between students, teachers, and parents), pedagogy (engaging practices), alterations in learning environments (wider and more interactive), and leveraging digital technology—all of which are in the service of the 6 Cs. We are finding that this has produced what we call "engaging the world, change the world," which has generated a whole new movement of students and teachers as change agents within their learning.

Much more detail, along with many concrete examples, can be found in *Deep Learning: Engage the World, Change the World* (Fullan, Quinn, & McEachen, 2018). Our main point here is that deep learning also changes the nature of leadership. Although it still requires coherence-making and the Competencies, the leadership role is more dynamic. Figure 5.4 contains the list of attributes of leadership for deep learning that emerged in the work of Fullan, Quinn, and McEachen (2018).

FIGURE 5.4

Leadership for Deep Learning

1. Cycles of trying things and making meaning
2. Co-learning among all dominates.
3. Leaders listen, learn, and ask questions.
4. Leaders help crystalize, articulate, and provide feedback on what they see.
5. Leaders act on emerging solutions, including a focus on impact.

We believe that our coherence-makers and the competency-equipped leaders on whom we have focused in this book are especially suited for this new work of deepening learning—the key to educational improvement for the future. The need for leadership of the kind that we have been portraying has never been greater or timelier. Coherence-making is a never-ending proposition. Leading learning and learning leadership are indeed one and the same.

References

Boston Consulting Group. (2014). *Teachers know best: Teachers' views on professional development*. Retrieved from https://s3.amazonaws.com/edtech-production/reports /Gates-PDMarketResearch-Dec5.pdf

Brooks, D. (2018, March 12). *Good leaders make good schools*. Retrieved from www.nytimes .com/2018/03/12/opinion/good-leaders-schools.html

Bryk, A., & Schneider, B. L. (2004). *Trust in schools: A core resource for improvement*. New York: Russell Sage Foundation.

Campbell, D., & Fullan, M. (In press). *Local governance in education: Its nature and potential*. Thousand Oaks, CA: Corwin.

David, J. L. & Talbert, J. E. (2013). *Turning around a high-poverty district: Learning from Sanger*. San Francisco: S.H. Cowell Foundation. Retrieved from http://shcowell.org /wp-content/uploads/2015/12/Learning-From-Sanger.pdf

Elmore, R. (2004). *School reform from the inside out*. Cambridge, MS: Harvard University Press.

Fullan, M. (2010). *All systems go*. Thousand Oaks, CA: Corwin.

Fullan, M. (2013). *Motion leadership in action*. Thousand Oaks, CA: Corwin.

Fullan, M. (2014). *The principal: Three keys to maximizing impact*. San Francisco: Jossey-Bass.

Fullan, M. (2017). *Indelible leadership: Always leave them learning*. Thousand Oaks, CA: Corwin.

Fullan, M. (2019). *Nuance: Why some leaders succeed and others fail*. Thousand Oaks, CA: Corwin.

Fullan, M. & Boyle, A. (2014). *Big-city school reforms: Lesson from New York, Toronto, and London*. New York, Teachers College Press.

Fullan, M., & Edwards, M. A. (2017). *The power of unstoppable momentum: Key drivers to revolutionize your district*. Bloomington, IN: Solution Tree.

Fullan, M. & Hargreaves, A. (2016). *Bringing the profession back in*. Oxford, OH: Learning Forward. Retrived from https://learningforward.org/docs/default-source/pdf/bringing -the-profession-back-in.pdf

Fullan, M., & Pinchot, M. (2018). The fast track to sustainable turnaround. *Educational Leadership, 75*(6), 48–54.

Fullan, M., & Quinn, J. (2016). *Coherence: The right drivers in action for schools, districts, and systems*. Thousand Oaks, CA: Corwin.

Fullan, M., Quinn, J., & Adam, E. (2016). *The taking action guide to building coherence in schools, districs, and systems*. Thousand Oaks, CA: Corwin.

Fullan, M., Quinn, J., & McEachen, J. (2018). *Deep learning: Engage the world, change the world*. Thousand Oaks, CA: Corwin.

Hargreaves, A., & Fullan, M. (2012). *Professional capital: Transforming teaching in every school*. New York: Teachers College Press.

Hargreaves, A., & O'Connor, M.T. (2018). *Collaborative Professionalism: When teaching together means learning for all*. Thousand Oaks, CA: Corwin.

Kirtman, L. (2014). *Leadership and teams: The missing piece of the educational reform puzzle*. Upper Saddle River, NJ: Pearson Education.

Kirtman, L., & Fullan, M. (2016). *Leadership: Key competencies for whole-system change*. Bloomington, IN: Solution Tree.

Knowles, M. S. (1988). *The modern practice of adult education: From pedagogy to andragogy*. Boston: Cambridge Book Company.

Kotter, J. P. (2008). *A sense of urgency*. Boston: Harvard Business Press.

Mehta, J. (2015). *The allure of order: High hopes, dashed expectations, and the troubled quest to remake American schooling*. New York: Oxford University Press.

Mintzberg, H. (2008). *Managers not MBAs: A hard look at the soft practice of managing and management development*. Oakland, CA: Berrett-Koehler Publishers.

Pfeffer, J., & Sutton, R. I. (2006). *Hard facts, dangerous half-truths, and total nonsense*. Boston: Harvard Business School Press.

Rose, T. (2017). *The end of average: How we succeed in a world that values sameness*. New York: HarperCollins.

Shaw, G. B. (n.d.). Quote retrieved from https://www.brainyquote.com/quotes/george _bernard_shaw_385438

Index

trust cycle, 23*f*
    predictability and, 24
    shared understanding and, 23–24
    teamwork and, 25

union leadership
    collaboration with, 79–80

vulnerability
    discussing mutual, 76

Whittier Union High School District, 40

York Region District School Board,
    38–39

About the Authors

Michael Fullan, OC, is the former Dean of the Ontario Institute for Studies in Education and Professor Emeritus of the University of Toronto. He is co-leader of the New Pedagogies for Deep Learning global initiative (npdl.global). Recognized as a worldwide authority on educational reform, he advises policymakers and local leaders on how to achieve the moral purpose of all children learning. Fullan received the Order of Canada (OC) in December 2012. He holds honorary doctorates from several universities around the world.

Fullan is a prolific, award-winning author whose books have been published in many languages. His latest books are: *The Principal: Three Keys for Maximizing Impact*; *Coherence: Putting the Right Drivers in Action* (with Joanne Quinn); *Deep Learning: Engage the World, Change the World* (with Joanne Quinn and Joanne McEachen); *Surreal Change: The Real Life of Transforming Public Education* (autobiography); *Core Governance* (with Davis Campbell); and *Nuance: Why Some Leaders Succeed and Others Fail*. For more information on books, articles, and videos, please go to www.michaelfullan.ca.

Lyle Kirtman has been a leadership development consultant for more than 30 years. As CEO of Future Management Systems Inc., he has worked on developing leaders to increase results for students in 350 school districts in 15 states. Kirtman's publications are influencing educators nationally and internationally. His books,

Leadership and Teams: The Missing Piece of the Educational Reform Puzzle and *Leadership: Key Competencies for Whole System Change* (Fullan) have influenced educational practice throughout the United States.

Kirtman's focus on innovation in education is a key element of his presentations, keynotes, and publications. He was able to help former Governor Patrick in Massachusetts by chairing the Governor's strategic planning task force on innovation in education. Kirtman brings a unique background to his leadership work in education through his consulting experience in the federal government (EPA), health care (Massachusetts General Hospital), universities (Harvard University), and in the corporate (Cisco Systems) and nonprofit (United Way) worlds. He has also worked as a senior administrator in the central office for the Boston Public Schools in the organizational development and leadership field for school operations.

Kirtman's field-based research has already made major contributions to the educational leadership arena through his 7 Competencies for Highly Effective Leaders, the use of leadership assessments for self-reflection and hiring, and the importance of getting a *C* in compliance to increase focus on results for student achievement.

Kirtman earned a bachelor's degree in psychology from the State University of New York (SUNY) and a master's degree in counseling with a concentration in career development from SUNY and Fairfield University, Connecticut.

Related ASCD Resources

At the time of publication, the following resources were available (ASCD stock numbers appear in parentheses):

Print Products

Leading High-Performance School Systems: Lessons from the World's Best by Marc Tucker (#118055)

Fighting for Change in Your School: How to Avoid Fads and Focus on Substance by Harvey Alvy (#117007)

Leading Change Together: Developing Educator Capacity Within Schools and Systems by Eleanor Drago-Severson, Jessica Blum-DeStefano (#117027)

Dream Team: A Practical Playbook to Help Innovative Educators Change Schools by Aaron Tait, Dave Faulkner (#119022)

Leading with Focus: Elevating the Essentials for School and District Improvement by Mike Schmoker (#116024)

Focus: Elevating the Essentials to Radically Improve Student Learning, 2nd Edition by Mike Schmoker (#118044)

Connecting Leadership with Learning: A Framework for Reflection, Planning, and Action by Michael A. Copland and Michael S. Knapp (#105003)

Changing the Way You Teach: Improving the Way Students Learn by Giselle Martin-Kniep and Joanne Picone-Zocchia (#108001)

Implementing the Framework for Teaching in Enhancing Professional Practice by Charlotte Danielson, Darlene Axtell, Paula Bevan, Bernadette Cleland, Candi McKay, Elaine Phillips, and Karyn Wright (#109047)

For up-to-date information about ASCD resources, go to www.ascd.org. You can search the complete archives of Educational Leadership at www.ascd.org/el.

ASCD myTeachSource®

Download resources from a professional learning platform with hundreds of research-based best practices and tools for your classroom at http://myteach source.ascd.org/.

For more information, send an e-mail to member@ascd.org; call 1-800-933-2723 or 703-578-9600; send a fax to 703-575-5400; or write to Information Services, ASCD, 1703 N. Beauregard St., Alexandria, VA 22311-1714 USA.

WHOLE CHILD
TENETS

The ASCD Whole Child approach is an effort to transition from a focus on narrowly defined academic achievement to one that promotes the long-term development and success of all children. Through this approach, ASCD supports educators, families, community members, and policymakers as they move from a vision about educating the whole child to sustainable, collaborative actions.

Coherent School Leadership relates to the **engaged**, **supported**, and **challenged** tenets.

For more about the ASCD Whole Child approach,
visit ***www.ascd.org/wholechild.***

1 HEALTHY
Each student enters school healthy and learns about and practices a healthy lifestyle.

2 SAFE
Each student learns in an environment that is physically and emotionally safe for students and adults.

3 ENGAGED
Each student is actively engaged in learning and is connected to the school and broader community.

4 SUPPORTED
Each student has access to personalized learning and is supported by qualified, caring adults.

5 CHALLENGED
Each student is challenged academically and prepared for success in college or further study and for employment and participation in a global environment.

LEARN. TEACH. LEAD.